P9-EDC-306

DEDICATION:
To all Porsche mechanics
and metal finishing specialists that are committed to the proper
care and repair of Porsche automobiles.

SIXTH EDITION, First Printing

Copyright 1999 by PMZ Publications

All rights reserved. No part of this book may be reproduced
or transmitted in any form by any means without the prior written permission of the author.

Manufactured in the United States of America

ISBN 0-9670442-0-0

Library of Congress Catalog Card Number 81-7003

PMZ Publications
720 Colorado Avenue
Santa Monica, CA 90401-2610

PROLOGUE

This publication is meant to be a basic, easy reading manual of value to those people planning on selling or purchasing a second-hand Porsche 911. Resale values will not be mentioned because of the tremendous variance in value from one geographic area to another. Many years of first-hand experience have led to the opinions and conclusions contained within this manual. These opinions are not intended to be the last word on the subject matter being discussed and are open for debate with interested parties. Unlike other publications concentrating on the Porsche automobile, this book does not make any attempt at avoiding discussion of the author's perception of weak points, or negative aspects, of certain models and years of manufacture. Because this is a presentation of the author's personal opinion to paint a complete picture, Mr. Zimmermann, Zimmermann Publications, or PMZ Publications, is not responsible in any way for any effect this book may have on the resaleability of any particular Porsche model.

The reader must keep in mind that only the models legally brought into the United States, as well as models suitable for daily use, will be covered in this manual. Also, many variables that involve optional equipment offered on certain models won't be discussed, but should be taken into account by both buyer and seller. The reason for this is simple—to most people, a 911 with a factory sunroof and factory air conditioning would be worth more than a "plain-jane" model, but a "hard-core" enthusiast might prefer the model with no extras fitted, and consider it a true "driver's car." Options are only worth what a buyer is willing to spend on them, and fully-loaded 911s generally don't sell for much more than models fitted with a limited selection of extras.

ABOUT THE AUTHOR

Peter Zimmermann's love affair with Porsche automobiles began in the late 1950's. Every publication that gave the slightest hint of containing information on the marque was purchased, read thoroughly, and sometimes memorized. Growing up in a household whose garage was usually occupied by Volkswagen Beetles, Porsche was destined to become the next logical step. The author purchased his first Porsche, a champagne-yellow 1964 356SC coupe, in 1967, and shortly thereafter became an apprentice mechanic for a small independent garage in Los Angeles. During this period, the 1964 SC was sold for a white 1958 Speedster, and as mechanical knowledge was gradually acquired, the urge to move on became overwhelming. The change was made, after a short stint at managing a service station, to a larger Porsche repair shop, also located in Los Angeles. The early seventies were spent acquiring technical publications, extensive 911 experience, and almost endless self-taught techniques of locating and solving problems within the 911 automobile.

The period from 1975 to mid-1976 included shop experience at an authorized Porsche-Audi dealership and considerable formal training in Porsche maintenance. June 1976 marked the opening of Red Line Service, Inc., co-founded by the author and one partner. This exclusive Porsche repair shop, located in Santa Monica, California, has grown into one of the nation's most respected repair facilities, and is a leader in the repair of 356 to 993 models.

The author is a twenty-seven year member of the Porsche Club of America (PCA), and has served as the Technical Director for the Los Angeles region. He also is a long time member of Porsche Owners Club, and the Sports Car Club of America (SCCA). After extensive experience competing in Porsche Club high speed events, Red Line Service built and prepared a Porsche 914/4 for SCCA E/P events, and the author drove this car to the California Club Regional Championship in 1985, winning six of that season's last eight races, and setting two lap records along the way. The author can be seen on the cover of this book playing at speed with his #67 911SC PCA club racer at Willow Springs International Raceway in California.

Red Line Service has remained at its original location, and for many years has offered a comprehensive range of services, including engine and transmission repair/overhaul, complete electrical and fuel injection repair, and, of course, scheduled maintenance for all 911, 928 and 944 models. Even with exposure to various water cooled Porsche models, as well as most non-Porsche contemporary automobiles, the 911 remains the author's first automotive love.

The Used 911 Story

Excellence was hoped for, but...

Table of Contents

Note: this book was written to provide a basic education on buying a used 911. Because some issues cover a range of model years, it is important to read the whole book—not just skip straight to the chapter detailing the car you're looking at.

More important, you may find, as you read through this book that the year and model of Porsche you were initially attracted to may not be the one that will give you the best ownership and driving experience.

Basic Checks

Before beginning the search for a second-hand 911, a potential buyer must make a priority list. To insure satisfaction after the purchase, this list should be adhered-to as closely as possible. Contrary to popular belief, exterior color is not important. A case in point is a customer of mine who purchased an extremely nice 1973½ 911T a while back. An acquaintance of ours approached the proud 911 owner and, after ten or fifteen minutes of careful scrutiny, remarked, "It's a beautiful car, too bad it's such an ugly color!" Well, after many years of perfect service and much enjoyment, the owner of this particular 911 has even gotten used to its color.

A priority list is fairly easy to make, once a person has ten or fifteen years of experience with Porsches. The following list, complete with explanations, is a good guideline to follow.

1. **Chassis:** The chassis, including suspension attachment points, must be near perfect. Minor imperfections, such as a small dent in a non-critical area, below the seats, etc., won't hurt a thing. On early cars, most noticeable on 1965 through 1968 models, the undercoating has a tendency to flake away in pieces. This is not a terminal problem provided the metal beneath is solid and unaffected. Surface rust is natural in these areas and can be eliminated successfully using a variety of methods prior to undercoating.

Picture #1

No metal deterioration may be present at rear torsion bar tube and jack point areas. The torsion bar tube (see picture #1) is a horizontal tube approximately three inches in diameter that extends left to right under the car just above and forward of the nose of the transmission. It is welded (see pictures #2 and #3) to the main chassis section beneath the rear seat area of the car. The jack points (see picture #4) are the

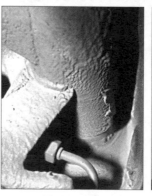

Picture #2

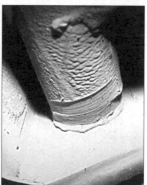

Picture #3

RED LINE SERVICE, INC.
720 Colorado Ave.
Santa Monica, Ca. 90401

3902

☐ SERVICE ☐ INSTALL	☐ WILL CALL ☐ DELIVER	PHONE	DATE	6/15/99

NAME Cash		APT.	MAKE	
			MODEL	
			SERIAL	

ITEM TO BE SERVICED	NATURE OF SERVICE REQUEST

QUAN.		DESCRIPTION OF PARTS OR MATERIAL	AMOUNT	
1		Used 911 Story	21	95

LABOR PERFORMED:		
Paid	Total Material	21 95
	Tax	
	Total Labor	
	Shipping	4 00
	Total Amount	25 95

DATE WANTED	DEPOSIT $	REC'D. BY

ESTIMATES ARE FOR LABOR ONLY, MATERIAL ADDITIONAL. WE WILL NOT BE RESPONSIBLE FOR LOSS, OR DAMAGE CAUSED BY FIRE, THEFT, TESTING OR ANY OTHER CAUSES BEYOND OUR CONTROL.

REPAIR ORDER   DUPLICATE

AUTHORIZED BY:

4K 455
REDIFORM®

TERMS - NET CASH
NO GOODS HELD OVER 30 DAYS

QUAN.	PART NO.	MATERIAL RECORD	PRICE EACH	AMOUNT		COST	
Outside Work							
			Total				

DATE	MECHANIC	LABOR RECORD	HOURS	RATE	AMOUNT	
			Total			

SUMMARY	COST		SUMMARY	SELL	
Total Material and Outside Work			Total Material and Outside Work		
Total Labor			Total Labor		
Total			**Total**		

Picture #4

receptacles in which the car's jack is inserted when needed.

One area of the chassis that is not necessarily a tip off on the car's general condition is the pan surrounding the fuel tank. The lower control arms (see pictures #5, #6, #7 and #8) bolt to this pan. If it is rusted badly (see pic-

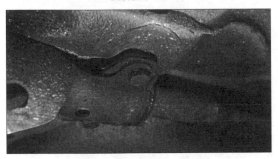

Picture #5

Picture #6

Picture #7

Picture #8

tures #9, #10, #11 and #12), beware! But if the rest of the chassis is satisfactory, it could simply mean that this car has had an overfilled battery (or batteries), or a faulty voltage regulator. In both cases, acid overflow could have caused the problem rather than too much winter, salted roads, etc. A cure for this problem is available. Hand fabricated pieces are O.K., but generally are very poor aesthetically. When factory parts are used and the work is carried out by a professional coach builder, this problem can usually be corrected for less than two thousand dollars. *Important:* always have the suspension re-aligned after a repair of this type.

An additional note on rust. A small ice-pick can be a 911 buyer's best friend. I have seen chassis rust cover-ups that were almost beyond belief. One such car, a 1967 911S, comes vividly to mind. This car was so bad

Picture #9

Picture #10

Picture #11

Picture #12

underneath that some enterprising soul had taken sections of thin cardboard, secured them over bad areas with duct tape, and then undercoated the entire chassis. It looked great, believe it or not, but my first tip off to its true condition was that our hoist moved an additional inch and a half, after initial contact, before that poor 911 moved upwards. The ice pick did the rest! A gentle push in suspect areas will reveal metal that is severely rusted, or worse, not even there any more. I must mention here that chassis rust problems in cars built since 1976, due to new production techniques being used during production, are extremely rare. Have the inspection done anyway, you never know what will be found!

Provided the chassis passes the rust test, it's not home free yet. It also has to be straight. Only a quality alignment shop familiar with Porsches can give the information needed here, but a very good test can be made with the help of a friend or seller of the car. With someone driving the car being checked, use another car to follow it. Speed is not important here. Thirty miles per hour is sufficient. While following from a distance of five to ten car lengths, sight down its sides. This will take some side to side maneuvering. Do it carefully. While sighting down the left side, for example, if a portion of the front tire can be seen protruding out past the rear tire, but while sighting down the right side the front tire CAN'T be seen past the rear tire, odds are good the 911 has been hit in the right front or left rear, and the entire chassis has been twisted counterclockwise. In some cases, this situation could be remedied, but it's hardly worth the bother, let alone the price.

There is no shortage of quality used 911s in the world, so patience should be exercised until a rust-free, undamaged chassis can be found. The chassis is by far the toughest area of the car to have repaired correctly, and probably the most expensive. It has to rank number one on my priority list, simply because it is the area of the car that in the final analysis will determine the quality level of the entire product.

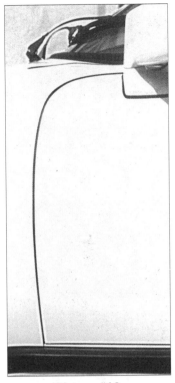

Picture #13

2. **Body:** Looking at bodies is generally a pleasant experience. The first thing to check is the seams (see pictures #13 and #14). Seams are the openings between the trunk lid and front fenders, the engine lid and rear quarter panels and, of course, the opening that surrounds each door. These seams must be of consistent

Picture #14

7

Picture #15

Picture #16

width and must be consistent with one another. Often, an irregular seam, upon closer inspection, will reveal improperly finished body filler. This filler will generally be a plastic auto body filler used by most body repair shops. A metal finisher using lead as a filler is usually more talented in the body repair art, and will finish seams properly prior to painting.

For example, uneven seams on the rear and right sides would probably indicate an impact in the right rear of the car. Seam variation can be a tremendous help in determining the level of damage sustained by a particular car.

Doors of a 911 should close lightly, without rattles or creaks. If a snapping or cracking noise is heard at the lead edge of a door, it is likely that the door stop (see picture #15), that part that prevents the door from swinging out too far on its hinges, is failing. These stops are inexpensive and should be replaced when bad, because a 911 door, if allowed to swing past its stop, may actually crease itself vertically along the exterior skin. Door jambs (see pictures #16 and #17) must be well finished and the paint surface free of overspray, runs, and rust.

The door jamb in picture #17 shows two decals that are applied at the factory during construction of the automobile. The top sticker is simply a "catalyst" decal seen on 1978 and later models. This means the car requires a catalytic converter to meet emissions standards. The lower decal is the important one, containing federal information, including the VIN (see page 18). This decal went into use in the model year 1970, and

Picture #17

is still used today. When this sticker is not present, it is advisable to look more closely for accident damage in that area of the car, for it is obvious that this part of the car has been repainted.

Engine and trunk lids should stay up by themselves, but if they don't, replacement of the small black cylinders attached to the hinges, two in front and one in the rear (most models equipped with a rear spoiler have two), will be necessary. These lids require different closing techniques. The front should close with a gentle push, using hands spread about six inches from each side of center (see picture #18), after the secondary latch has been engaged. Closing the engine lid is even easier. With the lid about a foot away from the closed position, a gentle shove in the center of the rear intake air grille (see picture #19) should be sufficient. Be sure to lift your hand away from the lid, or touch it only on the intake air grille, before it latches. This is extremely important on 1974 and later models. There are no more "Porsche" letters to strengthen the lid, and I have seen numerous cars that were near faultless with the exception of dents in the exact area those letters used to be. If the lids won't close as described, adjustment of the latches will be necessary.

One last test, a revealing one, that anyone can do effectively is sighting down the sides of the car. This should be done during daylight hours. The ideal place to do this is with the car in a garage. The main garage door should be open and

Picture #18

Picture #19

garage lights should be off. Then, by looking from the interior of the garage (see pictures #20 and #21), down the sides of the car, out toward the daylight, you will immediately see every ripple and imperfection in the car. Every problem

Picture #20

Picture #21

area seen means an increase in the next body shop bill.

3. **Interior:** Originality is highly desirable in this area. Taking just cost of repair into account, this item would be number four on the list. It has become number three based on the fact that there are far too few specialty upholstery shops available to have repair work done correctly. Headliners have to have the correct hole spacing and hues in the material. Side panels are very tricky to sew as original. I have seen so many "rebuilt" seats that don't feel like Porsche seats any more, that I would consider replacement with Recaros, or used originals, before having mine redone. Recaros will not hurt resale value and, in some cases, actually improve it. Carpet kits have flooded the market, but none that I have seen to date can match the quality of a custom cut and sewn installation done by a quality Porsche upholstery shop.

As with chassis and body, condition of the interior plays an extremely large part in the final selling price of any Porsche. With originality in all three categories present, the car will most certainly sell for top dollar. Anything that is non-original or done improperly can be used as bargaining power by the buyer.

4. **Drivetrain:** The drivetrain, in most instances, will require a larger expendi-

ture than the interior, but it is number four because of two reasons. One is the accessibility of quality repair. Two is that more often than not, a buyer is better off purchasing a car with overhauled drivetrain components rather than one with "original" units. The latter statement will be clarified in the section where the strengths and weaknesses of each model are discussed. There are competent (and not so competent) Porsche repair facilities within reasonable driving range of almost any major city. It is up to the potential buyer of a 911 to carefully screen different shops to decide which one will have the privilege of working on his car. When used properly, this manual can arm its readers with enough information to judge the competency of a shop, as well as its willingness to do the final checkout on a 911 that passes all the cursory checks.

One drivetrain check a buyer should always perform, or have performed, is a leak down test. This is a sophisticated compression check designed to not only reveal a potential problem but to pinpoint it. It will show an experienced user a burned valve, a ring problem or burned piston, etc. With each piston, in turn, put on top dead center, the spark plug for that cylinder is removed, and the hose for the leak down tester is put in its place. With a predetermined amount of air put through the machine and into the combustion chamber, the tester measures the amount of air escaping past various components of the chamber. If 100 psi of air pressure is applied through the tester, and the chamber holds only 75 psi, the result is 25% leakage. A good 911 will have readings in the 3% to 6% range. The factory maximum allowable figure is 10%.

The clutch is the least expensive "heavy" drivetrain repair but, at 1999 prices, can get up into the nine hundred to twenty two hundred dollar range on some late model 911s. One check, for oil contamination on the clutch assembly, caused by a faulty oil seal, can be made easily. Place the car on a slight incline and engage the clutch in a normal manner. If severe chatter (jerking) is felt as the clutch pedal is being let out, the car probably has an oiled clutch.[1] Engine removal is necessary to correct this, and may end up being a complete clutch re-placement. The other clutch check is for slippage. With the car properly warmed up and rolling forward in second gear, use full throttle to near redline on the tachometer, shift positively into third, and re-apply full throttle. If the tachometer shows a rapid gain in rpm but the car doesn't gain a commensurate amount of

[1]See "1975" 911's

11

speed, the clutch is either worn out, or has one or more damaged components. As before, removal of the engine will be necessary to repair the problem.

The transmission is a difficult component to analyze and can be done only by highly trained and experienced Porsche mechanics. Because Porsche automobiles require technique to be driven correctly, the following points will be kept basic. With the car warm, the engine idling, the radio off, and the windows closed tightly, there should be no obvious change in noise during release and depression of the clutch pedal. If the clutch pedal is depressed slowly and a far away whirring or growling noise begins about three quarters of the way in, odds are very good the throwout bearing is faulty. If the clutch pedal is depressed all the way and then released very slowly and a growling noise begins with the pedal about halfway out, the car probably has one or more bad transmission bearings. The throwout bearing repair does not require transmission disassembly, but transmission bearing repair does. If unusual noises are heard with the clutch pedal in either position, always obtain an expert's opinion. Another check for bearing failure may be done while driving. Using about four thousand rpm as a shift point, proceed up through the gears using no more than half throttle. If a distinct growl becomes more noticeable in each higher gear, relatively quiet in first to quite noisy in fourth and fifth, chances are that the pinion shaft bearing in the transmission has failed. This happens to be a characteristic problem in the 100,000 mile range of 1971 and earlier models, but is very rare on 1972 and later cars. Please read chapter entitled "911SC Continued..."

Gear synchronization problems can be related to technique and familiarity, so anything suspect concerning shifting should always be checked carefully by an expert.

Transmission ills can usually be cured in the twelve hundred to seventeen hundred dollar range, but much higher repair bills are possible. I'll stress this one more time – if anything about the transmission seems amiss, have the transmission specialist at a Porsche repair facility check it thoroughly.

5. **General Checks:** Looking at the car from the side, with it on level ground, should reveal a very slight downward forward "rake." The 911 automobile has a tendency to squat in the rear under heavy throttle, and with the front slightly lower to begin with, the car will maintain a more level attitude exiting turns and

during other maneuvers requiring acceleration. An entire book could be written about ride height and suspension settings, but, as a rule of thumb, a 911 should never be lower in the rear than the front, and there should always be space visible between the top of the rear tire and the bottom lip of the wheel opening in the quarter panel.[2] Basically, this space insures the car will not be too low, because reduced suspension travel, past a certain point, can produce hazardous results. Yes, this also applies to cars being autocrossed or time trialed.

Tire wear is very easy to check visually. Any cupping or rough areas on the tread surface will require a trip to the alignment shop and/or replacement of the shock absorbers. Do not treat this lightly. Tires and shocks are expensive. It is not unusual to pay, at 1999 prices, in excess of nine hundred dollars for four tires, and between six hundred fifty to seven hundred fifty dollars for a set of new shocks.

Brakes should not "pull" to one side, or exhibit any other frightening characteristics. They should not need to be pumped to gain good pedal feel, and they should not produce a cyclic pulsing at the pedal or the steering wheel during low speed (below twenty miles per hour) stops. A good way to save four hundred fifty dollars is to lift the carpet section from the driver's side floor and feel the underside of it as close to the throttle pedal as possible. If it is wet, odds are very good the car needs a new master cylinder, and replacement of the pedal cluster bush-

ings may also be necessary. The most common failure of the tandem master cylinder used between 1968 and 1976 involves leakage of brake fluid past the rear seal. The fluid runs down the brake pedal actuating rod and drips onto the cross shaft for the brake pedal. It then soaks the nylon-like material of the pedal bushings, causing them to expand and tighten on the brake and clutch shafts. In advanced cases, the brake pedal may be applied, and to release the brakes one must place a toe under the pedal and manually pull it back. From 1977 on, 911s

Picture #22

[2]The rear fender of the 911 is actually a quarter panel. That means the panel is welded rather than bolted in place.

have power brakes, identifiable on models built through 1989, by the power brake booster and fluid reservoir shown in picture #22. This unit is located under a layer of carpet in the trunk compartment. Failure symptoms range from a hard pedal to leakage of fluid under the brake booster, and sometimes the "brake" light, near the radio on the dashboard, will activate. If this light is on, the brake system should be checked as soon as possible.

All lights, stereo equipment, and other electrical accessories should be checked completely. A buyer can run through this entire procedure in less than an hour, and that one hour can save as much money as a round-trip plane fare to Hawaii!

NOTES

Purchase Worksheet

This chart may be helpful in deciding just how good the car being examined really is.

	1	2	3	4	5
Paint/Body					
Electrical					
Interior					
Wheels/Tires					
Trunk					
Stereo					
Other					

Definitions of the above numbers: (1) wreck, (2) poor, (3) average, (4) nice, (5) excellent.

For example, rating the body/paint section could be done as follows: A "1" would be a car that has dents/flaws in every panel, perhaps flaking/peeling paint, maybe some primer spots (as in picture #23). It could also have enough seam variation to arouse suspicion that the car has had at least one fairly serious acci-dent. A "2" would be a car in the same condition without seam variation. A "3" would be a car that is all one color, but could have fairly serious "road rash" (stone chips) across the front end, some small door dings, and maybe a small dent. A "3" is a

Picture #23

car that might look pretty good from twenty feet away. A "4" could be a car with light road rash, but no door dings or actual dents. There is still a good deal of reflective quality to the paint, which is still vibrant. A "5", of course, is a car that may cause your mouth to hang open for a minute, and then utter the word "wow". It will be a car with no obvious flaws, will be properly detailed, and will cause you to reach for your checkbook.

The interior may be rated the same way. A "1" would be a car that has springs poking through the seat fabric, if there is any seat fabric left, that is. The dashboard will resemble the floor of the Grand Canyon, the headliner will be torn and stained, and the carpeting will be in a sad state, and might smell like a cat lives in the car. A "2" is a car in the same condition as the "1", but all the parts are still intact, although heavily worn. A "3" could earn its rating by having an intact headliner, seats with no tears, functional door pockets, and carpets that could be improved by vacuuming. A "4" would be a car that is actually pretty nice, doesn't have any cracks in the dashboard or tears in the fabric, and the headliner is clean. The vinyl/leather can show some minor wear or scuffing, but the car is definitely nice enough to take your significant other to dinner in. A "5" will be a car that looks like it's never been sat in, smoked in, parked in the sun, etc. and will give you the impression that you don't have to fear what might be under the seats if you buy the car.

The other categories listed, and any additional ones you might want to add, can be broken down the same way. When you total up the points and divide by the number of categories, you will know how good the car is that you're looking at.

Once a car passes these inspections, it is ready for a thorough pre-purchase inspection by your friendly local Porsche service shop to assess the engine, transmission, suspension, brakes, chassis, and provide a second opinion on your ratings of the other areas of the car.

V.I.N.

VIN=Vehicle Identification Number.

These numbers are generally used for registration purposes, although on some older cars an engine number may be found on the registration and ownership documents. When production of the 1965 911 began, Porsche merely continued the numbering system that had been used for the 356 series. The first 1965 911 carried the chassis number 300001, and all 911s built thru the end of the model year 1967 had consecutive numbers beginning at that point. In 1968, a new system was initiated where each digit, or group of digits, had a specific meaning. The new VIN had eight digits for the 1968 models. The breakdown of a typical 1968 911 chassis number may be found on the opposite page, diagram 1.

The VIN was changed again for the model year 1969. It was increased to nine digits, each of which are defined in diagram 2.

Beginning with the 1970 models, thru the end of the 1979 model year, Porsche used a ten digit VIN described in diagrams 3 thru 8.

The 1980 models saw yet another VIN revision, and an analysis of these numbers may be found in diagram 9.

A drastic VIN change took place in 1981, and for these models, diagram 10, should be studied. Generally, the VIN can be found on the vehicle by looking through the windshield inboard of the left side "A" pillar, as shown in picture #24, or on the left door jamb, picture #25. The "world producer code" is an identification code for every manufacturer, and Porsche's code is "WPO". The "VDS" code consists of two letters and one number. The first letter tells which series (911, 924, 928, etc.) the car is. The letter A is used to depict a 911 coupe or a 924, the letter E is used for

Picture #24   Picture #25

Targas and the letter J is used for 928s. The second letter tells what engine type is in that particular car. Diagram 11, on page 21, further explains this letter. The third digit of the VDS code describes the restraint system in the vehicle; "0" stands for "active" and "9" stands for "passive".

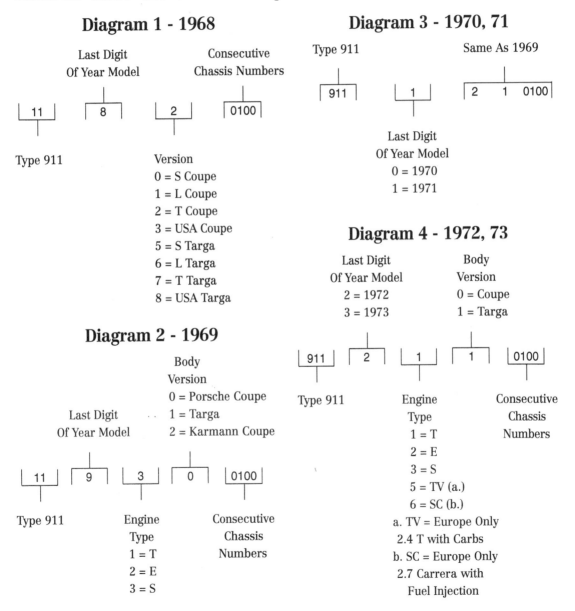

Diagram 1 - 1968

Last Digit Of Year Model

Consecutive Chassis Numbers

| 11 | 8 | 2 | 0100 |

Type 911

Version
0 = S Coupe
1 = L Coupe
2 = T Coupe
3 = USA Coupe
5 = S Targa
6 = L Targa
7 = T Targa
8 = USA Targa

Diagram 2 - 1969

Body Version
0 = Porsche Coupe
1 = Targa
2 = Karmann Coupe

Last Digit Of Year Model

| 11 | 9 | 3 | 0 | 0100 |

Type 911

Engine Type
1 = T
2 = E
3 = S

Consecutive Chassis Numbers

Diagram 3 - 1970, 71

Type 911   Same As 1969

| 911 | 1 | | 2 | 1 | 0100 |

Last Digit Of Year Model
0 = 1970
1 = 1971

Diagram 4 - 1972, 73

Last Digit Of Year Model
2 = 1972
3 = 1973

Body Version
0 = Coupe
1 = Targa

| 911 | 2 | 1 | 1 | 0100 |

Type 911

Engine Type
1 = T
2 = E
3 = S
5 = TV (a.)
6 = SC (b.)
a. TV = Europe Only
2.4 T with Carbs
b. SC = Europe Only
2.7 Carrera with
Fuel Injection

Consecutive Chassis Numbers

19

Diagram 5 - 1974

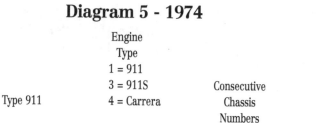

Engine
Type
1 = 911
3 = 911S
4 = Carrera

Type 911

Consecutive
Chassis
Numbers

| 911 | 4 | 3 | 1 | 0100 |

Last Digit
Of Year Model

Body
Version
0 = Coupe
1 = Targa

Diagram 7 - 1976, 77

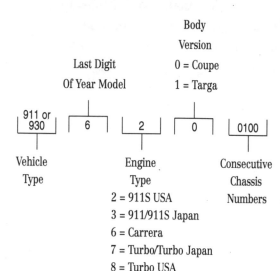

Body
Version
0 = Coupe
1 = Targa

Last Digit
Of Year Model

| 911 or 930 | 6 | 2 | 0 | 0100 |

Vehicle
Type

Engine
Type
2 = 911S USA
3 = 911/911S Japan
6 = Carrera
7 = Turbo/Turbo Japan
8 = Turbo USA

Consecutive
Chassis
Numbers

Diagram 6 - 1975

Body
Version
0 = Coupe
1 = Targa

Last Digit
Of Year Model

| 911 | 5 | 2 | 1 | 0100 |

Type 911
(930 = Turbo)

Engine
Type
1 = 911
2 = 911S USA
3 = 911S
4 = Carrera USA
6 = Carrera
7 = Turbo

Consecutive
Chassis
Numbers

Diagram 8 - 1978, 79

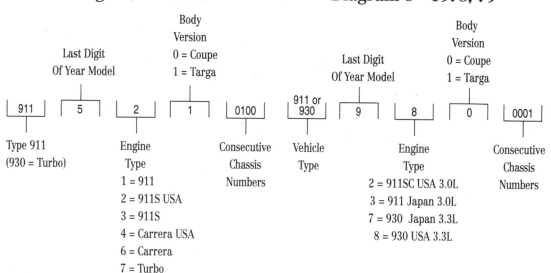

Body
Version
0 = Coupe
1 = Targa

Last Digit
Of Year Model

| 911 or 930 | 9 | 8 | 0 | 0001 |

Vehicle
Type

Engine
Type
2 = 911SC USA 3.0L
3 = 911 Japan 3.0L
7 = 930 Japan 3.3L
8 = 930 USA 3.3L

Consecutive
Chassis
Numbers

Diagram 9 - 1980

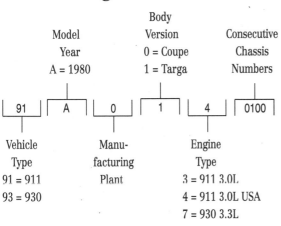

Vehicle Type
91 = 911
93 = 930

Model Year
A = 1980

Manu-facturing Plant

Body Version
0 = Coupe
1 = Targa

Engine Type
3 = 911 3.0L
4 = 911 3.0L USA
7 = 930 3.3L

Consecutive Chassis Numbers

| 91 | A | 0 | 1 | 4 | 0100 |

The last word on VIN is perhaps the most important. Always, without fail, have the local police or highway patrol check the numbers to make sure the vehicle is not stolen!

Diagram 10 - 1981-on

| WPO | AAO | 91 | 0 | B | S | 1 | 2 | 0001 |
| a. | b. | c. | d. | e. | f. | g. | h. | i. |

a. World Producer Code
b. VDS Code
c. 91 = 911/93 = 930
d. Test Digit
e. Model Year (B = 1981, C = 1982, D = 1983, etc.)
f. Manufacturer Location Type (S = Stuttgart)
g. 3rd Digit of Porsche Type (1 = 911, 0 = 930)
h. Body/Engine Code
    2 = 911 SC Coupe USA/Canada
    5 = 930 Turbo Canada
    6 = 911 SC Targa USA/Canada
i. Consecutive Chassis Numbers

Diagram 11 - VDS Code

Code	Attributes	911	924	924 Turbo	928
A	Fuel	GAS	GAS	GAS	GAS
	Cylinders	6	4	4	8
	Displacement	2994	1984	1984	4478
	Horsepower	172	98	110	220
	Manufacturer	Porsche	Porsche	Porsche	Porsche

Engine Number

The 911 has been around for more than thirty years now, so there have been instances when abuse or neglect have created a situation where an engine swap may have financially been the better solution to a problem involving engine failure in a number of Porsches still running. When a swap takes place, it is not always done well, and not always done using like parts, so using an engine number to correctly identify an installed unit could pay dividends. For example, if the car being inspected is a 1975 911S, and is fitted with a 1970 911T engine, it will not be able to pass its required smog checks for registration purposes. It will also have fifty less horsepower, much less torque, and will need tuning more frequently! Not exactly a bargain, no matter how you look at it. The engine number (see pictures #26 and #27) is located to the right of, and below, the cooling fan, on a vertical boss, and faces to the rear, on very early aluminum cases, and to the right on all cases built to date. Near this number, on a horizontal surface approximately 2½ inches forward of the engine number is a second number. This one (see picture #28) is an internal designation code, which enables one to tell what the particular engine actually was when assembled at the factory, by supplying more information than the engine number can by itself. For example, the 911/44 shown is the designation for a 1975 911S engine manufactured for use in California, which tells us that the engine was originally equipped with thermal reactors as part of the emission control system. For comparison purposes, a 911/43 crankcase is one manufactured for use in all states except California, and, as a result, was fitted with a different exhaust system, consisting of two heat exchangers and a primary muffler, and no thermal reactors. Always try to locate this number and call your favorite Porsche expert to have it identified. When the vehicle identification number (VIN), the engine number, and the internal designation number are all available, and match, the car being checked is prob-

Picture #26

Picture #27

ably going to be a better one than a
911 that has had an engine swap.
Of course, there are always exceptions to the rule. One scenario
could be that the 911 being checked for purchase is a 1975 Carrera,
and it has a 1976 911S engine
number. Let's say this car had a
valve job at 55,000 miles, and did
not have case savers installed as
part of the repair. 15,000 miles
later the cylinder heads began to
loosen, and the engine was taken apart again, for case savers. Unfortunately, the

Picture #28

savers were not done in a precision manner, as outlined in the engine overhaul
chapter in this manual, but the engine seemed okay following assembly, so was
returned to daily use. 30,000 miles passed by, and the loose cylinder head symptom returned, and was confirmed during a visit to the repair facility. Sensing
something was being missed, the car's owner went in search of a different, more
technically oriented, shop for a second opinion. Upon disassembly, this shop found
the poorly installed case savers, which damaged the case beyond repair, and
determined that a used, re-conditioned case was the best way to handle this
repair. No 1975 Carrera case could be found, so the alternative was a 1976 911S
case in good condition. Shop number two then had case savers correctly installed,
and using all of the components of the original engine, along with the replacement case, built a good engine for the car. The car now has 140,000 miles on it,
runs perfectly, and has no loose cylinder head symptoms, which makes it a perfect candidate for resale, even with a non-matching engine number. This type of
history is entirely possible, but one should always demand receipts when the
engine numbers don't match the VIN. Please use the charts on pages 24 through
26 to determine that everything is as it should be with the Porsche you're thinking
about buying, and if you happen to find a number that doesn't appear in the
charts, you should contact your favorite Porsche expert to further analyze that
number.

Diagram 12

Year: 1965
900001 - 903550   130 HP - 911 w/Solex Carbs
Year: 1966
903551 - 907000   130 HP - 911 w/Solex Carbs
907001 - 909000   130 HP - 911 w/Weber Carbs
Year: 1967
909001 - 911000   130 HP - 911 w/Weber Carbs
911001 - 912050   130 HP - 911 w/Weber Carbs
                            New Cams/Exhaust
960001 - 962178   160 HP - 911S

Diagram 14
Year: 1969-71 Example: 6200001

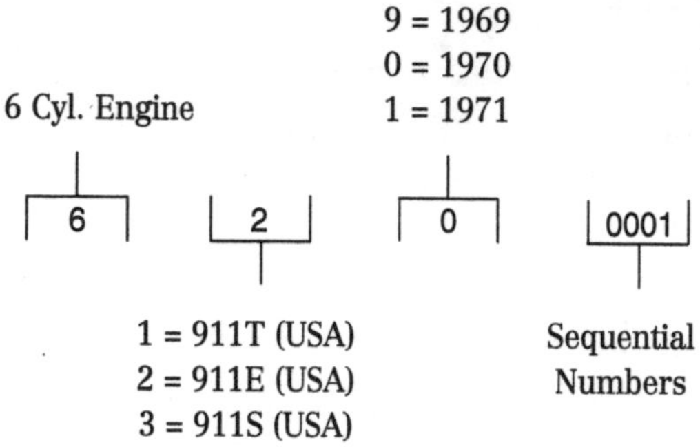

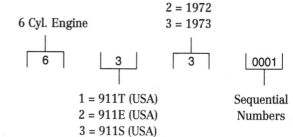

9 = 1969
0 = 1970
1 = 1971

6 Cyl. Engine

6   2   0   0001

1 = 911T (USA)
2 = 911E (USA)
3 = 911S (USA)

Sequential
Numbers

Diagram 13
Year: 1968   Example: 3280001

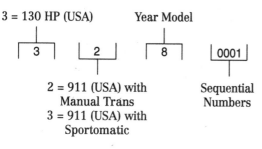

3 = 130 HP (USA)   Year Model

3   2   8   0001

2 = 911 (USA) with
    Manual Trans
3 = 911 (USA) with
    Sportomatic

Sequential
Numbers

Diagram 15
Year: 1972-73 Example: 6330001

2 = 1972
3 = 1973

6 Cyl. Engine

6   3   3   0001

1 = 911T (USA)
2 = 911E (USA)
3 = 911S (USA)

Sequential
Numbers

Diagram 16
Year: 1974-75 Example: 6140001

6 Cyl. Engine

4 = 1974
5 = 1975

| 6 | 1 | 4 | 0001 |

'74: 1 = 911 (USA)
    3 = 911S/Carrera (USA)
'75: 4 = 911S/Carrera (USA)
    5 = 911S/Carrera (Calif)

Sequential
Numbers

Diagram 18
Year: 1978-79 Example: 6890001

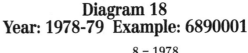

6 Cyl. Engine

8 = 1978
9 = 1979

| 6 | 8 | 9 | 0001 |

2 = 911SC (USA)
5 = 911SC (Calif)
8 = Turbo (USA)

Sequential
Numbers

Diagram 17
Year: 1976-77 Example: 6460001

6 Cyl. Engine

6 = 1976
7 = 1977

| 6 | 4 | 6 | 0001 |

'76: 4 = 911S (USA)
    5 = 911S (Calif)
    8 = Turbo (USA)
'77: 2 = 911S (USA)
    8 = Turbo (USA)

Sequential
Numbers

Diagram 19
Year: 1980-81 Example: 6400001

6 Cyl. Engine

0 = 1980
1 = 1981

| 6 | 4 | 0 | 0001 |

4 = 911SC (USA)

Sequential
Numbers

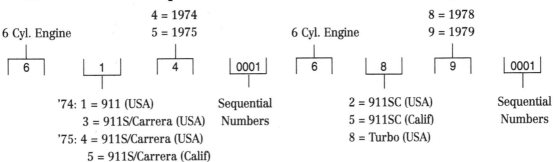

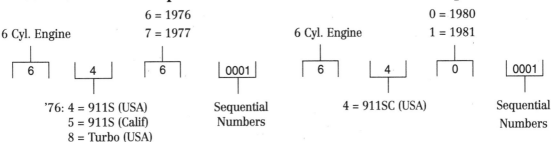

Diagram 20
Year: 1982-83 Example: 64C0001

6 Cyl. Engine

C = 1982
D = 1983

| 6 | | 4 | | C | | 0001 |

4 = 911SC (USA)

Sequential
Numbers

Diagram 22
Year: 1986-89 Example: 68G00001

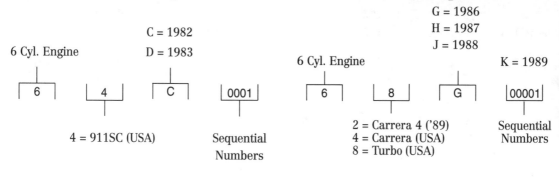

G = 1986
H = 1987
J = 1988

6 Cyl. Engine

K = 1989

| 6 | | 8 | | G | | 00001 |

2 = Carrera 4 ('89)
4 = Carrera (USA)
8 = Turbo (USA)

Sequential
Numbers

Diagram 21
Year: 1984-85 Example: 64E00001

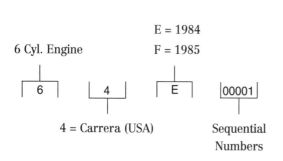

6 Cyl. Engine

E = 1984
F = 1985

| 6 | | 4 | | E | | 00001 |

4 = Carrera (USA)

Sequential
Numbers

Diagram 23
Year: 1990-93 Example: 62L00001

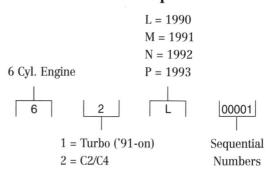

L = 1990
M = 1991
N = 1992

6 Cyl. Engine

P = 1993

| 6 | | 2 | | L | | 00001 |

1 = Turbo ('91-on)
2 = C2/C4

Sequential
Numbers

NOTES

1965/1966

Contrary to popular belief, there is a 1965 911. As a matter of fact, there are quite a few. Unfortunately, most of them have terminal rust problems or have gone to the graveyard for other reasons, as have the '66s. The two model years have been grouped together here because they are almost identical. The "911" designation represents the only model, and the engine was a two-liter capacity, somewhat "peaky" power plant. When I say "peaky", I'm referring to an engine that actually is somewhat slow at low rpms, and then at 4,000 rpm, the car comes alive and accelerates much more briskly. Acceleration was outstanding for such small displacement, the five-speed transmission was very smooth, and once mastered, an absolute joy to use. The shift pattern has first gear where I think it should be, to the left and back. All 911 five-speeds used this pattern through 1971, and all 914s and 928s use it also. Handling characteristics require patience and practice to become used to because oversteer[1] happens quite suddenly. The short wheelbase[2], on all 1965 through 1968 models, tends to cause front to rear pitch that is not that noticeable on the 1969 and later models.

Some subtle differences between the 1965 and 1966 models are: (1) The ignition switch may have a solid brass retaining nut encircling the key receptacle on a 1965 model, while the 1966 model has a large diameter black plastic retainer. (2) The 1965 will not have vinyl trim at the extreme left and right ends of the wooden section of the dashboard, while the 1966 will. (3) The 1965 and 1966 (through mid-year) models were fitted with Solex carburetors, while the late 1966s were equipped with Webers.

One curiosity of the 1965 and 1966 models is that the wiper blades "park" on the right side of the windshield, opposite of every other model except for 1967.

One very expensive repair needed on these models is the changeover from Nadella to Lobro rear half axles. The Nadella is easily spotted (see picture #29), for it has exposed

Picture #29

[1]Oversteer is a term used to describe a car's handling characteristics when the car has a tendency, when driven hard, for the back end to slide while the front remains stable.

[2]The distance between the front and rear wheel centers is referred to as wheelbase. This distance was lengthened by an additional 55 millimeters in 1969.

"U" joints, while the Lobro has rubber dust boots at its ends. A car with Lobro axles on it already is definitely a plus, as is one that has been changed over from Solexes to Webers. Solexes are terrific, but they are extremely difficult to set up properly and are prone to wear out throttle shafts[3] prematurely. This wear ruined their reputation and, unfortunately, most mechanics won't take the time to set them up properly. Some years ago, I drove a 1965 911 for about 40,000 miles and, after spending about thirty hours on the carbs at the time of purchase, I did not have to readjust them once for the remainder of the time I owned the car!

Early 911s, 1965 through 1968, as well as some 1969s, were not equipped with a capacitive discharge ignition[4] system (commonly referred to as a "CD" unit). This CD unit's job is to increase voltage at the spark plug, thereby extending effective spark plug life from about 1000 miles to well past 6000 miles. When I speak of "effective" plug life, I mean that the vehicle in question can still accelerate to redline in fourth gear without a trace of misfire. There are those that claim they are getting 25,000 miles to a set of plugs, but that is a lot of bunk. There surely isn't a carbureted 911 in existence that doesn't need new spark plugs at least every 10,000 to 12,000 miles. Anyway, an early 911 that already has an aftermarket or factory CD unit installed is a plus because, although its price isn't bad (most units can be installed for less than $400), its presence may indicate a car owner that cares enough about the car to improve it sensibly.

> *Summation:* The 1965 and 1966 911s are a terrific car, but they are now old enough to make extreme care in purchasing one an absolute necessity. I restored a 1966 911 from the ground up for myself in 1977. The project took the better part of a year, and customer cost of the project would have been over $13,000. When the cost of repair far exceeds the resale potential of the vehicle, the restoration of the vehicle in question normally ceases to be a good idea. An enthusiast that is purchasing a sound, strong early 911 may have to look long and hard for the right car.

[3]Throttle shafts are those shafts that pass through the base of the carburetor's body and hold the butterflys in place. A butterfly is a round metal disc in the carburetor that opens and closes during throttle applications, allowing air to flow into the engine.
[4]All models from 1969 on are equipped from the factory with some form of electronic ignition system except for the 1969 911T. In this vehicle, it was a factory option.

1967

A very special 911 in the minds of many. The engine was still two liters displacement, but some changes were significant. This marked the first year of the 911S. The regular 911 was almost unchanged from 1966. The wood dash was gone forever, but there were no other obvious visual changes. The 911S had an increase of approximately thirty horsepower over the 911, and both cars were equipped with Weber carburetors and five speed transmissions. A sight to behold was a brand new 911S fitted with what has become one of the 911's most familiar trademarks, the factory forged aluminum alloy wheel. Shown in pictures #30, 31 and 32 are some variations of what have become known as "factory alloys". Picture #30 is a 6 x 15" wheel with factory finish. Picture #31 is a 7 x 16" wheel, also with a factory finish, but in poor condition. Picture #32 is a 8 x 16" wheel finished in L.A. glitter, ah, chrome. Factory alloys have been finished/painted in

Picture #30

Picture #31

Picture #32

almost every imaginable way, which serves to emphasize their enduring style.

The first ones were only four and a half inches in width, compared to the seven inch wheels on the rear of the 911SCs. The narrow wheels were the direct result of the tire manufacturer's inability to produce a wide tire that had good anti-hydroplane[1] qualities in wet weather. As the tires became better, the rims became wider, and wet, as well as dry, handling progressed measurably.

The 911S was, in many people's opinion, the first street Porsche to give that true "race car" feeling of acceleration. Applying full throttle at 3500 rpm felt like any other car, but at 4500 rpm, wow! A definite surge of power causes the car to leap forward, and when it's time to shift, just above 7000 rpm, the whole exhilarating process repeats itself. I have never driven a small displacement vehicle made by any other company that can come close to matching the acceleration of the 1967 S.

This was also the first year of the Targa. The first Targas were made in both 911 and 911S models, and were equipped the same as the coupes. The rear window of the 1967 and 1968 Targas was a zip-out affair that, when combined with top removal, gave a true convertible feel. Install the top, zip up the rear window, turn on the heater, and the car is transformed from an open sports car to a warm, comfortable, weather-proof touring car-an interesting concept that is still in production today, and has been copied in one form or another by many other manufacturers.

> *Summation:* Everything said about the 1965 and 1966s holds true here. If a 1967 911 or 911S can be found in top cosmetic and mechanical condition, it is a rare find indeed.

---

[1]The tendency a tire has to actually lift up and lose contact with the road surface, and actually ride on a sheet of water.

1968

To date, the 1968s are the most easily identifiable models, even from fifty feet away. They have reflectors, permanently attached to the sides of the car, that serve as side marker lights. These reflectors were eliminated for 1969, when the side markers became an integral component within the front and rear lamps.

The 911S, after only one year, disappeared from United States showrooms. It could not qualify within the parameters of clean air requirements, so the only models for 1968 were the 911 and 911L. 911L? The 911L was, simply, a standard 911 equipped with a luxury group. This group included forged alloy wheels, fancy interior appointments, and exterior "911S" trim.

1968 marked the year of the air injection (smog) pump. It was the only year that needed one until 1975, and to find a car with the pump system still functional would be highly unlikely. Registering one of these cars without a working pump may be difficult, because pollution control regulations in many states have become very tough. Always check this out with your local department of motor vehicles before purchasing the car!

An important development that appeared in 1968 was the Sportomatic transmission. This transmission employs a torque converter and clutch assembly that is automatically controlled electrically with an assist from vacuum. No clutch pedal is needed in these cars, because when a gear change is desired, a microswitch in the base of the gearshift lever senses movement at the lever and causes the clutch to disengage, putting the car in neutral, thus allowing the driver to select the appropriate gear. The torque converter allows the car to idle at rest, in gear, and then to accelerate from rest in true automatic transmission fashion. Although it is a "clutchless" four-speed, and not an automatic, it is extremely nice to use in commuter applications. Third gear, for example, may be used in zero to fifty applications without any shifting being necessary.

Certainly not a favorite with mechanics because of system complexity, the "Sporto" was an option through 1977 and definitely has its place in any Porsche story.

Summation: The 1968 911s have not gained any notoriety as a "special" model but can be just as satisfying to drive as any early 911. For these reasons, a good buy is possible because across the board resale values tend to be lower than the 1966 and 1967 models. If a Sportomatic is what one is looking for, a very good buy is possible because Sporto resale values are generally lower than comparable five-speed manual transmission models.

1969

911T, 911E, and 911S. Carburetors and fuel injection. Shocks and hydropneu-matic suspension. Six inch wide alloy wheels. New turn signal assemblies. Flared fenders. Stretched wheelbase. A year of change!

The 911T is a pleasant car that was offered in both four and five speed trans-mission versions, as were all of the 1969 models. The T is easy to remember concerning significance; just think of "tame." This car is wonderful for daily commuting or open highway use. Although performance isn't staggering, the 1969 T can be driven all day long at ninety miles per hour without effort, and still be very pleasant in urban use. The Weber carburetors are highly reliable and present no tuning difficulties. As usual, fit and finish were impeccable, both inside and out. The T, E, and S were all available in coupe and Targa form, but factory-installed sunroofs were still a rarity. All three models were also offered with an S package, including front and rear anti-sway bars, larger brakes, instrumentation that included an oil pressure and oil tank level gauge[1], oversize rubber trim on front and rear bumpers and special rocker panel treatment.

Like the T and S, the E received a subtle fender contour change in 1969. Both coupes and Targas now sported a slight flare at the wheel opening of the rear quarter panels and the front fenders. This flare not only allowed the use of the wide six inch wheels, but enhanced exterior appearance. Also, the lights at the four corners of the car changed in design. The early cars, 1965 through 1968, used a lamp that had the lens permanently attached. Obviously, it was an expen-sive proposition to replace an entire tail light, or front parking light, just to repair a cracked lens. From 1969 through 1989, lens' can be replaced without having to remove the lamp housing from the car. Removable lens' are easily identified by their three mounting screws, compared to only two screws on '68 and earlier cars. From the beginning of C2/C4 production, rear lamps only have one screw, and the entire assembly swings out to access bulbs.

The 911E was equipped with a front suspension system that, in time, has been proven virtually useless. It was called hydropneumatic suspension. Gone were the front shock absorbers and torsion bars. In their place was a hydro-pneumatic strut.

Hydropneumatic struts were self-leveling units designed to take the place of both the shock absorbers and the springs (torsion bars), and through the use of

[1]This instrumentation was standard equipment on all models prior to 1969.

gas and oil in high and low pressure chambers, give a ride that is extremely comfortable. All in all, it was a decent idea that was never really accepted by most Porsche people. This system was an option on T models, as well as being standard equipment on the E. Replacement hydropneumatic units are extremely expensive, roughly four times that of a shock absorber, so most often a car equipped with hydro units is converted to conventional shock and torsion bar units when one of the original hydro units fail. This conversion is also very expensive, but once it is done, shock replacement becomes a normal exercise, when required. The conversion can be done in most cases in its entirety for less than the purchase and installation of two new hydropneumatic units.

Another milestone in the development of Porsche 911s occurred in 1969. The E and S models were fitted with mechanical fuel injection, instead of the customary carburetors. In a nutshell, with this system, fuel is injected into the intake ports via injectors, while air is drawn in through velocity stacks. In theory, this system was the answer to all the world's problems. In practice, it was something less. Tuning of this system is extremely difficult and, when repair or replacement of components becomes necessary mechanical fuel injection is many more times as expensive as carburetion. Fuel economy, compared to other 911 models, is horrible, and smoothness has been sacrificed for performance. A gentle surging, or bucking, at steady speed or light throttle applications, is not unusual and can be considered "nature of the beast" in some models.

All 1969 models witnessed a major suspension change. The wheelbase, which is the distance between the center of the front wheel and the center of the rear wheel, was stretched from 221 to 227 centimeters. This change created a much more neutral handling car. it also produced a smoother ride by reducing the front to rear pitching motion that most short wheelbase cars are afflicted with.

> *Summation:* The 1969 models are the last of the 2.0 liter displacement models, are light feeling, easy to drive cars that are quick and fairly well mannered. A mediocre example may not be worth fooling with, but a nice, well maintained car could deliver years of good motoring.

1970 - 1971

These two years are grouped together because the cars are virtually identical. Some people believe these cars are the best 911s Porsche has ever built. I say they are not the best, but they are great. The engine displacement has been increased to

Picture #33

2.2 liters, the T still has carburetors, the E and S still have mechanical fuel injection, and the Es are still equipped with hydropneumatic suspension. From outward appearance, the easy way to tell these models from a 1969 are the exterior door handles. In 1969 Porsche used push buttons for the last time. Beginning with 1970, right through 1998, the door handles have a small pull lever concealed on the back side of the grab handles. 2.2 liter models were delivered with a beautiful rear window decal of a 911 engine with "2.2" written boldly through the center of it. These decals have virtually disappeared on anything short of a show car. The correct placement of the decal was bottom dead center.

The 1970 and 1971 911Ts (picture #33) were an absolute blessing. The car pictured has been fitted with a 1974/75 model outside rear view mirror for safety purposes. (the original mirror was round) but is otherwise an accurate depiction. Not many people realize just how good these cars were, and still are today. For all purpose use, both town and interstate, the car is just about the perfect blend of horsepower, gear ratios, economy, comfort, and quiet that has ever happened to sports car drivers. It can produce 25 miles per gallon at 85 miles per hour, can be driven all day long at 110, or can loaf along in town at 2800 rpm in any of the three lowest gears. These cars were good from day one, lots of them were sold, and nice examples are plentiful compared to most other models.

The only thing that spoiled the 2.2 911E, a good mannered horsepower car, is the hydropneumatic front suspension. Other than that, the E is a good, fast reliable car that, when in proper condition, can deliver as much satisfaction for your money than anything ten thousand dollars can buy today.

The 2.2 911S is a rocket! Release the clutch first, accelerate smoothly to 4500 rpm, shift into second, release the clutch, and plant the throttle pedal on the floor. Things happen quickly up to about 4700 rpm, and then from 5000 to 7000 rpm, wow! Some of the fastest cars on the road in 1971 were 2.2 911Ss. They are an absolute thrill to drive correctly, are very rare and, if in top dollar condition, will cost the buyer a fortune, and rightly so!

> *Summation:* Perhaps the best total line of 911s yet offered the buying public, the 2.2 liter cars have to be considered a 9 on a scale of 10.

914-6, 1970 - 1972

1970 witnessed the introduction of a funny looking little sports car, the 914. In the late '60s Porsche and Volkswagen had ties in some countries because of marketing agreements, Porsche was acting as VW's importer and distributor in Austria, and there was a marriage between children of the Nordoff (VW) and Piech (Porsche) families. These, and other connections between the two companies, led to discussions that eventually led to the production of the 914. An early agreement basically stated that Porsche would design and develop a mid-engine sports car for Volkswagen, based on a four cylinder engine already being developed for the VW type 411. In return they would be able to develop the car in a different direction to suit their own needs. The result was a car that did not look like a Porsche, but was acceptable to both companies. In order to provide adequate space for the anticipated mid-mounted six cylinder engine, as well as passengers, the car's wheel base was extended seven inches longer that the 911, but overall length was actually seven inches shorter than the 911. Although all 914s sold in the United States were marketed as Porsches, I'm only going to discuss the "6" here, because of its shared 911 drive train heritage. The car is a true two-seater, lightweight at approximately 2170 pounds, and fitted with the beautifully smooth 2.0 liter engine used in the 1969 911T. The transmission is a five speed unit, controlled by linkage that has to reach all the way to the rear of the car to do its job. The front suspension is taken from the 911, including wheel bearings and hubs that incorporate the five stud design for wheel mounting. The rear suspension is a trailing arm design that uses a coil-over spring/shock absorber system, and five stud hubs. Design elements that were intended to improve the look of these cars were vinyl covering on the sides of the roll bar (or rear roof quarters, if you prefer) trimmed with chrome, and chrome bumpers. Wheel choices ranged

Picture # 34

38

from 5.5 x 15 steel rims, to extremely light, attractive, die-cast magnesium units of the same size, and 5.5 x 14 Fuchs factory alloys that were a common option purchased for U. S. models. The 914/6 had a base price of about $6,000, and the same car today, in premium condition, will bring more than three times that amount. The reason for this is that very few of the original cars, out of a build total of 3360 units, remain, because many have been highly modified, or used in competition. The bulk of the cars were built in 1970, with a few '71s, most of which were intended for competition, to be used while the remaining inventory of the poor selling cars dwindled in supply, and production eventually stopped. Poor sales were the result of image, or lack thereof, a much to small price difference separating it from it's big brother, the 2.2 liter 911T, and relatively poor magazine write-ups. If they had only known what a small displacement increase, 911S cams, a front anti-roll bar, stiffer rear springs and 16" wheels would do for one of these cars!

> *Summation*: Although many design experiments were tried with the 914/6, among them the 914/6 GT, the 916, and the 914/8, the basic car remains as a fun to drive, responsive, decent stopping car. It is low, sporty and noisy, all of which many consider a true sports car should be, and a good one is going to be very hard to find.

1972

The beginning of "Wide World of Sports" reminds me of the transition from '71 to '72. Especially the quote, "The thrill of victory to the agony of defeat." 1972 was a very mixed-up year. The highly visible identifying trademark of these cars is the oil tank access flap, that looks exactly like a gasoline cap access flap, located on the forward part of the right side quarter panel. All 911 models to date have a dry sump lubrication system for the engine. This system requires a reserve oil tank located away from the engine. In every 911 built, until the 1989 Carrera 4, this oil tank is located behind the right rear wheel, just beneath the outer skin of the quarter panel, except for the 1972 models. Porsche placed the oil tank forward of the rear wheel in 1972 and, in so doing, provided a way to check and add oil without opening the engine lid of the vehicle. The access flap is opened with a push button located on the passenger side door jamb.

This year witnessed a major change in the transmission. It was the first year Porsche used an "H" pattern for 1st through 4th gears, and placed 5th all the way to the right and forward. Reverse is below fifth, to the right and back. All 911 5-speed models from 1972 to 1986 use this shift pattern. The redesigned transmission (picture #35) is very strong, but a little more "balky" to shift than the early (pre 1972) 911s. Although time has proven over and over again the reliability of this new transmission, the factory made, in 1972, what I consider a mistake. Every transmission in every Porsche ever built has a mainshaft seal. This seal is located in the area of the car, where the engine and transmission are bolted together, that houses the clutch and flywheel assembly. The mainshaft of the transmission protrudes from inside the transmission into the clutch housing, where it makes contact with the clutch disc. This is the way power is transferred from the engine, through the

Picture # 35

clutch, into the transmission and finally to the rear wheels, via the differential and rear axles. In order for the clutch to stay clean and dry, the mainshaft has to be sealed at its point of entry into the clutch housing. This is done with a mainshaft seal. The seal's only purpose in life is to make sure all the transmission fluid in the transmission stays in the transmission. If the seal fails, the clutch becomes contaminated with transmission fluid, and replacement of the clutch is necessary. In most Porsches built through 1986 this is a relatively simple task that can be performed in five to seven hours by simply removing the engine. Once the engine has been removed, the leaking mainshaft seal can be replaced, the clutch repaired as necessary, and the whole assembly reinstalled in the car. On 1972 models, the transmission has to be removed from the car and completely disassembled, because the mainshaft seal was installed from inside the transmission! Add about ten hours labor to the bill for this procedure.

1972 marked the end of the carbureted 911T. Displacement was increased to 2.4 liters on all models (by increasing crankshaft stroke for the first time) and mechanical fuel injection was added to the T. As a result, fuel consumption increased and the ultra smooth characteristics of the earlier Ts all but disappeared. Too bad! The E was a decent car overall, now that hydropneumatic suspension finally became an option, and the S was an unbelievable performance car.

Summation: The 2.4 liter 911S may be considered a very special car, although very costly to repair, but not too much can be said about the 1972 911T. Purchase of a car such as this should be considered very, very carefully with regard to price and exactly what is to be expected from the vehicle. The 911E may or may not fit your specific needs, they are far and few between, and rarely can be found in pristine condition. Unless the "perfect" 1972 911 can be found, it might be a good idea to look elsewhere.

1973

Everything that was said about the 1972s holds true for the early '73 models. Roughly the first third of 1973 911s produced had the peculiar mainshaft seal problem, the remainder of the 1973 models were fitted with a different clutch housing which allowed the seal to be replaced without a transmission tear down being necessary. The 1973 models are easily identified even from a distance, because of their rubber bumper guards. They are black in color, and protrude

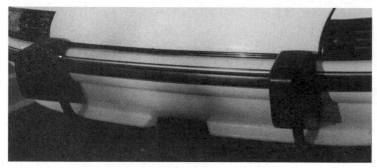

Picture #36

Picture #37

much further than the metal guards of past models. The guards are very narrow, and are incorporated into the same bumper system used in 1972 and earlier models (pictures #36 and 37). 1973 is the last year to use this bumper system.

1973 911s were fitted with an improved shift linkage that made the cars much nicer to drive.

Summation: What about the 1973½ 911T, one might ask? Please proceed to the next chapter. As for the 1973 911E or S, if one in exceptional condition can be found, it will probably cost a small fortune to purchase, and not be exactly cheap to operate. The car's fuel consumption rate is quite high, they are expensive to repair, but have a performance level virtually unmatched until the appearance of the 1976 930 Turbo Carrera.

1973½ 911T

Ah! Finally! Porsche builds their first "10"! This is one model that deserves its own chapter. A major breakthrough came with this car - "CIS" fuel injection. "CIS" means "Continuous Injection System". Another name for it is the Bosch terminology, "K-Jetronic". Basically, this system is not mechanical, and it is not electronic. It is a system that functions on pressure and vacuum. Simple to tune, this injection system is highly efficient, and may deliver in excess of thirty miles per gallon during highway operation. All the smoothness of the earlier carbureted 911s is back, plus some. All things considered, this is the smoothest, most pleasant of all 911s built to date to drive. The engine, at all rpm levels, is responsive and has sufficient torque to allow use of very low engine speeds in city applications. Even 2600 rpm, for example, is comfortable for second gear steady speed use.

The transmission is very smooth in these cars, and the mainshaft seal problem already discussed (under "1972" models) has been corrected, except in a few of the earliest models. The 2.4 liter displacement engine delivers enough horsepower and torque to enjoy almost any driving situation.

Fit and finish of the exterior, when the cars were new, was as good as any car could expect to be. Seams and paint were perfect, almost as though the folks at the Porsche factory knew they were building really special models. I've maintained a number of these 911Ts since they were new, some now have in excess of 150,000 miles on them, and no other 911 model has shown a lower "cost per mile" bottom line.

Summation: A very, very special 911!

1974

The 911T is history. The survivors are the 911, 911S and Carrera. 1974 saw a major change (for Porsche anyway) in exterior design. The bumpers were totally redesigned because of the 5 mph damage free contact requirement instituted by the federal government. The bumper configuration, still in use through 1989, took a long time for Porsche "old-timers", like myself,

Picture #38

to get used to, but the concept was well integrated with the body. In retrospect, they almost give the car a "grown up" look.

All 1974 models are fitted with "CIS" fuel injection, all are very smooth, with the S and Carrera being quite fast. Again, displacement has been increased, this time to 2.7 liters. Driveability of these cars is excellent, resale values are good, and their popularity rating is very high. The 2.7 liter engine, though plagued with certain problems (be sure to read "1975") was more reliable in 1974 than in 1975 or 1976. No add on smog control devices had yet appeared, and the engine compartment, for the last time until 1980, had a clean, straight-forward appearance.

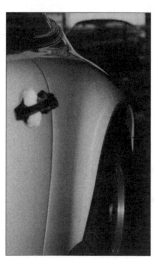

Picture #39

Identifying 1974 models from the back is quite easy-they are the only 911s ever built for the U.S.A. with narrow rear bumper guards (see picture #38). All 911 models from 1975 through 1989 use bumper guards at the rear that are approximately 7 inches wide, or about twice that of the 1974 guards.

From the front, it is virtually impossible to identify the different models between 1974 and 1977, the exception being the Carrera models. The 1974 Carrera received the first "flared" rear fenders (see picture #39), the exact contour used on all 1978 through 1989 non turbo-charged models, seven inch wide rear wheels fitted with

Picture #40   Picture #41

wider tires, and a distinctive rear spoiler that was part of the engine lid. This rear spoiler has been dubbed the "duck-tail", or "sugar-scoop", and was used only on 1974 Carrera models.

This year saw a major change in seating. The "throne" seats appeared for the first time and are in all 911 models, with minor improvements, to date. Side and thigh support was better with the new seats, and headrests became an integral part of the seatback. Door pockets no longer pulled out for loading (as in the 1969-1973 style shown in picture #40) but, instead, were fixed boxes with a flip-up top (picture #41). Very neat and convenient to use, they remain virtually unchanged today.

> *Summation:* The 1974 911s are still a very popular car, despite valve guide and intermediate shaft problems (see "1975"), and resale values are unusually high. The 911S and Carrera models are rare and command high prices, even those in mediocre condition. All the 1974 models are smooth, fun to drive, fast and have good torque for effortless city operation.

1975

The 1975 models were a product of the revised emission standards period. A myriad of problems plagued these cars and lower resale values have been the result. For example, revisions in the clutch release system resulted in clutch chatter when, in fact, there is nothing seriously wrong. However, the chatter is very annoying when starting out on a hill, backing up an incline, or even during routine operation. As another example, turn signal switches, at over two hundred dollars to replace, fail regularly. The high/low beam function of the switch is the weak point, and the problem can be repaired without switch replacement only by talented mechanics and only, even then, about fifty percent of the time.

The California models have just about every problem that any 911 has experienced to date, all rolled into one. This was the first year for thermal reactors to appear. They were necessary (in California), along with an air pump and an exhaust gas recirculation system, to make the car comply with clean air standards. Put briefly, thermal reactors cause a tremendous increase in exhaust temperature, nicely burning up unburned hydrocarbons arriving from the exhaust ports. Unfortunately, they also cause a tremendous amount of heat directly below the cylinders and cylinder heads. This heat causes a myriad of oil leaks from "fried" oil seals, o-rings and non-gasketed surfaces. These oil leaks are extremely expensive to repair, and as long as the reactors are left intact, are also repetitive. They are not nearly as expensive, however, as replacement of the valve guides, which also deteriorate from heat at extremely low mileage. I have seen this particular repair done as early as thirty-five thousand miles, and the resultant bill was over three thousand dollars!

Unfortunately, (there's that word again) things begin to snowball at this point. Let's just say we are examining a beautiful 1975 911S (or Carrera) with about 45,000 miles, documented, on the odometer. The car seems to have excessive valve noise, as well as a cyclic grinding noise at low rpm in the center of the engine, but the leakdown test (discussed in the "Basic Checks" section) percentages are okay. An additional test may be made. Drive the car for about the length of a city block at a steady 4,000 rpm, and then release the throttle completely. If a white cloud from the exhaust pipe follows the car to a stop, the car has serious valve guide problems. The grinding noise is generally caused by a worn out or damaged intermediate shaft. This shaft is about six inches long, has a gear in the center that is driven by the crankshaft, and two sprockets on which the timing chains ride. These chains, in turn, drive the left and right camshafts of the engine. The center gear is the component of the shaft assembly that wears out, allowing backlash, which in turn creates noise.

During repair of the car's engine, the following will take place.

Picture #42

1. Remove engine from vehicle.

2. Remove all intake and exhaust components.

3. Remove all valve train components, including the cylinder heads (see picture #42).

4. Remove cylinders to determine piston ring wear in the compression ring grove.

5. Measure cylinders for roundness.

Picture #43

6. Disassemble engine case, crankshaft assembly and (see pictures #43, #44 and #45) hardware from the engine case and install thread inserts. This permits proper re-torquing of the cylinder heads during installation, and is only necessary on engines of the 2.7 liter family (1974 through 1977) or modified performance engines using cases manufactured between 1968 and 1977.

Picture #44

7. Measure and check every component, and reassemble engine using new parts where applicable. The bottom line for all

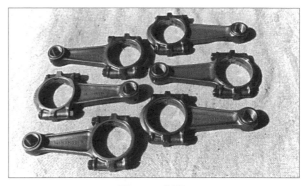

Picture #45

47

this is usually in the eight thousand plus dollar range.

Eight thousand dollars! Whew! One very nice result of all this, provided the car can be purchased at a good price, and if the repair is done correctly, and if the 1975 copper valve guides are replaced by higher quality bronze guides, and if thermal reactors[1] (on California cars) are eliminated, is that the "new" engine should now last one hundred thousand miles or more with proper care and maintenance.

Transmissions are very good in the 1975 models, and have shown no weaknesses to date. Interiors are holding up very well, fit and finish of the body is excellent, and paint is also very nice. Handling characteristics, ride comfort, tire wear and brake system component life expectancy are all normal.

> *Summation:* The 1975 911S or Carrera (a stunningly beautiful car) can be transformed into a precise, reliable automobile but, if the engine problems mentioned have not been cleared up, the car is sure to be a trouble maker.

---

[1]Thermal reactors may be replaced with "headers" manufactured and sold by many after market parts outlets, or an entire "49 States" model exhaust system can be installed. In California, both changes are illegal.

1976

A model without much change, the 1976 911S was the only 911 brought in to the United States with one exception, the Turbo Carrera. As for the 911S, few changes were made from 1975.

One of the most obvious was the elimination of the hand throttle, previously located to the immediate left of the emergency brake handle, that was necessary for starting the car according to the owners manual for each individual model. In 1976, Porsche adapted an automatic system which allowed the driver to just turn the key and drive away, regardless of ambient or engine temperature. The cars are somewhat "balky" after a cold start, but generally smooth out in less than thirty seconds. The automatic starting system is still used to date, although many changes have taken place in the form of refinements.

Unfortunately, all the engine problems that plagued the 1975 911 models hold true for the '76s. California cars still come equipped with thermal reactors, and cylinder heads were still fitted with inferior valve guides. Displacement remained unchanged at 2.7 liters, and performance was approximately the same as the 1975 911S. Premature engine failure has hurt the reputation of the 1976 models, and resale values have suffered as a result.

One minor change can be found directly in front of the driver. The speedometer, to this day, is now electronic, rather than cable driven off the transmission, as were all 911 models from 1975 back. The 1976 models were the first models to sport outside rearview mirrors color coordinated to the car. These mirrors are electrically adjustable and have electric defrost capability. All 911 models through 1991, except for the '91 Turbo, come equipped with these mirrors, the one on the right side being optional through 1979.

Although mechanical changes were few, one of the most important changes ever to be made, not only at the Porsche works, but in the entire auto industry, took place for the 1976 models. Very few people are aware of it, but these models, sold in West Germany, were delivered with a full six year unconditional warranty covering any and all rust or corrosion damage to the basic chassis unit excluding the fenders. The reason this amazing warranty was possible was that all sheet steel pieces of the assembly were first coated with zinc, using a hot galvanizing process, before final assembly. This warranty is not valid in the United States, but all 911 models built since early in the 1976 model year have had the same treatment done to their basic steel parts, so rusty 911s from 1976 on will be far and few between.

>   *Summation:* 1976 models were just average cars (for Porsche that is), but if one can be found in nice condition, and has already had engine repairs taken care of, it would certainly be worth while taking a closer look at.

930 aka 911 Turbo

During the fall season of 1975 a new and delightful beast arrived at our shores. It had huge fender flares (picture #46), and seven and eight inch wide by fifteen inch diameter forged alloy wheels. A rear spoiler that was soon dubbed the whale tail, and a front spoiler, made from rubber, that extended below the front bumper. It had the insignia "Turbo Carrera" fastened to the engine lid, and the logo *turbo* written in the carpet on the back of the left rear jump seat. The car was built with standard equipment such as full leather interior, air conditioning, stereo, an automatic heater control system and tinted windows. The

Picture #46

option list was short, with the two most popular items being sunroof and limited slip differential. The feeling I got from looking at one of these cars up on a lube rack was surpassed only by the experience of driving one.

Zero to sixty acceleration times can be discussed and compared until one is blue in the face, but no standard production car legally imported into the United States at the time, could match the performance of the Turbo Carrera. The Turbo should be driven very, very carefully initially. It requires the maximum attention and respect a person can give it. The car should have been sold with a special prerequisite of having attended a professional driving school prior to ownership. It is difficult to describe how quickly things happen in one of these cars, because it all occurs without the usual noise, wheelspin and fishtailing often associated with extremely fast cars. Turbos just cover large expanses of real estate in very short periods of time! Even Danny Ongais reportedly once said that he only drives his 930 fast in a straight line.

1977: The 930, still called Turbo Carrera, saw some interesting changes. These were the first cars to be delivered with Pirelli P7 tires mounted on sixteen inch diameter forged alloy wheels. The width of these new wheels remained at seven inches on the front, and eight inches on the rear. Because of this change, handling qualities improved noticeably.

Another change was the mounting method for the wastegate. The wastegate is a spring-loaded valve that, when turbocharger pressure builds to a specified level, opens to divert the exhaust flow to the muffler. This wastegate was troublesome in the 1976 models, often failing in less than three thousand miles because the wastegate was mounted horizontally, permitting exhaust system condensation to attack the valve. To correct this, Porsche engineers relocated the wastegate slightly to allow for moisture drainage, and at the same time upgraded the valve material to stainless steel. The wastegate is now reliable for twenty thousand miles and more.

The tachometer was changed to allow the addition of a bar gauge in the bottom center of the instrument. One bar is a unit of measurement that is approximately fourteen pounds per square inch of pressure. This bar gauge is commonly referred to as a "boost" gauge, and measures turbocharger pressure at the intake manifold.

A very important modification was made to 1977 models, both the 930s and the 911s, involving the brakes. Porsche gave them a power assist that made a world of difference in pedal feel and effortless stopping. All subsequent 930 and 911 models built until C2/C4 production began, use this system, with a brake caliper change on the 930s beginning with the 1978 models.

1978: These exotic West German autos underwent a name change in 1978. "Carrera" was dropped, and the cars were simply called "Turbo". Changes included new brake calipers and huge cross-drilled ventilated rotors, the addition of an intercooler and a larger whale tail. The brake calipers were similar to those used on the 917, have four pistons each, instead of two, and generate an incredible amount of pressure against the back side of the largest brake pads ever used on a street Porsche.

The intercooler is a radiator-like unit added to the turbo charging system that cools the pressurized

Picture #47

air between the turbo charger and the intake manifold. This insures only minimal power loss at higher operating temperatures. The unit is quite large, and is housed beneath the extra large whale tail, which is easily identified by the high vertical lip on the rubber outer section, shown in picture #47.

Perhaps the most important modification Porsche made for the 1978 model year was to increase the engine size from 3.0 to 3.3 liters. This change can actually be felt while driving, by one who is thoroughly familiar with Porsche's flagship. The extra torque at lower engine speeds makes the car easier to operate in heavy traffic situations, while a modified clutch makes initial movement smoother.

1979: Other than being the last production year, until 1986, for sale and use in the United States, the 1979 930s saw little change from 1978. A good deal of emphasis, for purposes of potentially increasing the resale value, has been placed on the last fifty serial numbers of the 1979 models, but the desire to own one of these cars has died down somewhat because various companies have been "federalizing" the 1980 through 1985 Turbos since the last fifty 1979 cars were originally sold.

1986: The return awaited by Turbo lovers throughout the United States finally took place. Porsche fitted a catalytic converter to the exhaust system of these cars, and along with other changes, was finally able to gain approval to sell the 911 Turbos here. One unfortunate aspect of the "new" Turbo is that the cars are still fitted with a four speed transmission, which is OK for open road use, but somewhat difficult to use in town, or heavy traffic. The 1986 models seem to have even more turbo "lag" than earlier models, and combined with the four speed, they are work to drive compared to Porsche's normally aspirated models. "Lag" is basically the period of time that passes while the rpms of the engine are increasing to the point where exhaust flow becomes sufficient to spin the turbocharger fast enough to produce "boost", which produces the afterburner effect. This boost, or rush of acceleration, normally happens at about 3800 rpm, which has been the single largest reason for all the aftermarket development of exhaust systems, larger turbos, larger intercoolers, camshaft experimentation, etc. The search for a lower boost point has been exhaustive, and that search has resulted in a variety of products that are now readily available that produce great gains in horsepower and torque, and some combinations will lower the boost point as much as 600 revs. Obviously, with all things good, there is usually a downside, and in this case it is the possibility of reduced reliability. Huge amounts of common sense must be used when driving a modified 911 Turbo, and extensive homework should be done prior to choosing the combination of items to be used in order to reach a desired goal, because it is easily possible to spend more than ten thousand dollars doing the project. The 1986 Turbos, like their little brother, received new anti-roll bars—22mm, instead of 20mm, in the front, and 20mm, instead of 18mm, in the rear—which has effectively reduced body roll without sacrificing ride comfort. They have also received the ventilation improvements of other 1986 models, and an increase in rear wheel width from 8" to 9", allowing the use of 245/45 x 16 tires, instead of the 225/50 x 16 units used on earlier models. Still fitted with what is basically the same 3.3 liter engine used since 1978, the 1986 Turbo is a smooth, quiet 911 with the same incredible ability to consume huge expanses of road in an almost casual fashion.

1989: Whoa! What about 1987 and 1988 turbos? Well, they are basically unchanged 1986 models, but in 1989 there was a major change. The 911 Turbo has finally received a five speed transmission! Coupled to the engine, still 3.3 liters in displacement, by a hydraulic clutch, the new five speed makes the 1989 Turbo the best one yet. "Lag" is less noticeable during town driving, because there is now a gear available for most traffic situations, compared to the four speed transmission, when the revs always seemed to high in second, or to low in third. The 1989 Turbo is a great car!

1990: The Turbo took 1990 off in preparation for the 1991 model, which saw major changes.

1991: The Turbo engine remains 3.3 liters in displacement, and the transmission is the same as the one developed for 1989, but the remainder of the car is based on the C2 platform. The suspension changes, as well as climate control improvements, a better stereo, and detail changes make the C2 Turbo a sensational car.

1994: After taking another year off, the 911 Turbo returned with a vengeance. For the first time since 1978 a displacement increase took place, this time to 3.6 liters. CIS was still the fuel injection of choice, and the manual transmission remains a five speed. This is the first 911 produced that received the huge brakes used until the end of '97 production, easily recognizable by the red calipers so prominent inside the beautiful three-piece Speedline wheels. This car is the first of the Turbos that accelerates exceptionally well in the lower rev ranges, and has absolutely stunning acceleration once the turbocharger kicks in. All in all, a remarkable car, to be succeeded by an even better one (please read "993").

1977

This was a year of few changes, but these changes formed a valuable link to the "SC" series that began in 1978. As in 1976, the only 911s imported were the 911S models and the Turbo Carreras.

This year saw an important mechanical development in an area that has not been discussed until now. 911s have always been plagued with one so called "weak link" in the engine-the chain tensioner. A chain tensioner (see picture #48) is a miniature hydraulic jack whose job is to retain proper tension, via an idler pulley, against the camshaft drive chain. The 911 engine has two camshafts, one for each half of the engine, therefore it has two chain tensioners. The tensioners are totally independent of one another, and do not have to be changed in pairs if one fails. For the record, the tensioner itself (and history has proven this many, many times) is not the true weak link in the design. Until 1977, the chain guide, or ramp, has been the real trouble maker. Each chain has three of these guides. They do what their name implies, they keep the chain on track between the chain drive sprocket and the tensioner actuated idler pulley. From 1968[1], these guides were made from a hard rubber material. This material (up until 1973) generally stayed flexible for 100,000 miles or more. From 1974, when

Picture #48

"lean burn" and smog devices began to take over, these guides became very hard and brittle. When a chain tensioner fails, it causes excessive chain movement, or whip, which in turn slaps at the guides. This slapping often breaks off guide ends, which then may travel up the chain, jamb between chain and sprocket, and cause chain breakage, bent valves and a myriad of associated problems. I consider the guides the true weak link because this guide breakage problem can also happen without the tensioner failing. When a tensioner fails, it will almost always occur below 3000 rpm, and will be very noticeable at idle, when the chain has almost no centrifugal force to help hold itself tight. The resulting noise is very hard to describe, but is a loud growl combined with the sensation that something within the engine has become very loose, and is contacting surrounding components. If this noise is ever experienced, no further driving should be

[1]1965-1967 chain guides were aluminum with vulcanized material on the face that contacted the chain. Failures were very rare, I personally have never seen one.

done. If the engine is shut off immediately and towed to a competent repair shop, no further work should be needed than replacement of the tensioner and its guides. The mistake 911 owners make is continuing to drive the car. This gives the loose chain an opportunity to beat against, and possibly break, its guides, causing extensive internal damage. Even from 1977 on, it's not a good idea to drive a 911 with a noisy tensioner, but at least guide breakage probably won't occur. New guides have been developed from a totally different material, and they work. We have taken 911s apart, just to check on these new units, and after 50,000 miles they are unchanged from new. There is no surface cracking or other forms of visible wear. Hopefully, beginning with 1977 models, the chain guide problem has been solved. (The new units may be retrofitted to all earlier 911s.) Chain tensioner development, please see 1984, has also been making progress, and late model tensioners, used through 1983, have been much more reliable than the units fitted to pre-1976 autos.

> *Summation:* Basically, the 1977 is a 1976 with the above described improvements, plus superior valve guide material. Engine life in a properly maintained 1977 should go well past 100,000 miles, which should be a welcome relief to Porsche owners worldwide.

1978

Rumor had it that a very special 911 was on the way, although every one in the business felt the 2.7 liter engine had been developed fully. The 1977 911s were quite good, and no one ever dreamed that in one model year such drastic improvement could be achieved. Many companies in the automotive industry are capable of major changes from one model year to the next, but I don't think it has ever been done to the extent that Porsche did it in September 1977. Suddenly, the cars being unloaded at the docks had 3.0 liter, aluminum alloy engines, instead of the 2.7 liter magnesium unit used the previous year. The cars also looked better, and more aggressive, with their flared rear quarter panels, like those of the 1974 Carrera, seven inch width rear wheels, and Pirelli P7 tires. A quick look under the back end of the car revealed a catalytic converter mounted outboard of the lower left valve cover. Finally! No more thermal reactors and excessive heat directly under the engine. A quick look under the right front fender revealed an auxiliary oil cooler on all models, with or without air conditioning. A quick look at the engine lid revealed a new emblem -"911SC".

Porsche must have known all along it would come to this. They just teased us with lesser versions of the ultimate car all these years. The last time the letters "SC" appeared on a Porsche were 1964 and 1965 356 C high performance models. These were superior automobiles compared to their predecessors. The 911SC certainly deserves its initials, because it is also superior to those that came before it.

Although not without fault, the 911SC is certainly the best of the 911s to date. Acceleration is very good. Handling is not exactly neutral, but excellent and totally controllable by capable drivers. The brakes defy comparison, when compared to other cars built between 1978 and 1983, and fit and finish is what one would expect in a $30,000 automobile.

The primary negative aspect of 911SCs is the clutch. It blows up! The rubber center, torque damper, of the clutch disc actually disintegrates to the point where the entire mechanism becomes inoperable. This disc has been improved at least once by Porsche,

Picture #49

58

and at this writing is supposed to be a long life unit beginning with the 1982 models. A sure cure for this problem is to use an improved clutch disc (see picture #49), part number 915 116 011 22, when replacement is needed. My shop has performed many repairs in this manner with a 100% customer satisfaction rate. Average life of the original equipment clutch, from our experience, is only about 25,000 miles, while more than a few clutches we have repaired are well past 60,000 miles with no need for replacement. Once the clutch problem has been taken care of, one would have a difficult time finding a sports/tourer (at any price) that even comes close to the 911SC in terms of performance, looks and reliability.

> *Summation:* The 911SCs, beginning with the 1978 model year, have proven to be incredibly reliable automobiles. Engine and transmission life should easily surpass 200,000 and 100,000 miles respectively, with proper care and maintenance. With the addition of a breakerless ignition distributor, used in all 930 models, the ignition system has become virtually maintenance free. Cold starting characteristics are acceptable, and warm, as well as hot, starts are perfect. Combine the reliability aspect with the fit and finish, as well as the performance, and the result is the best of the 911s.

911SC, Continued...

Basically, through the end of the 1983 model year, very few noticeable changes occurred but numerous improvements were made. In 1980, for instance, the fuel injection had an important addition referred to as the Lambda system. This system uses a probe in the exhaust system that senses information needed by an on board computer in order to alter, as necessary, the fuel/air ratio received by the engine. This insures a perfect mixture in all temperature conditions. The 1980 models have proven to be slightly unstable, often needing fuel injection calibration, and idle adjustment, between major maintenances, which are required every fifteen thousand miles. Each model year, after 1980, has shown increased stability, with the 1983 models being the best. Service costs of these cars increase somewhat, because at 30,000 miles it is required, in order to maintain an optimum state of tune, that the owner have the the previously mentioned exhaust probe, which is actually called an oxygen sensor, replaced. The labor to perform this task is minimal, but the cost of the part is approximately $110. Also, with the addition of the Lambda system, Porsche found that it was no longer necessary to use an air injection pump (smog pump), so the engine compartment became much cleaner, and mechanics always appreciate all the help they can get. One other change worth mentioning occurred in 1980, air conditioning became standard equipment on all models. Aftermarket air conditioning, generally speaking, had become so poor in so many ways (compressor mounting systems, hose routing, service accessibility) that Porsche finally did something about it and put factory air in all the cars sold through the dealer network in the United States.

1983 marked a fabulous introduction, the Cabriolet (see picture #50). Finally, 911 buyers could opt for a true convertible, instead of a Targa with the fixed back window. The Cabriolet is a beautifully engineered car, both with the top up or down. It is quieter than the Targa with the top up, except for engine

Picture #50

noise heard through the plastic back window, and more enjoyable, for convertible fans, with the top down. The heating system is easily up to the job of keeping the feet warm during evening, and nighttime cruising during spring, summer and fall months (in California, anyway), and is a wonderful car to both look at, and drive, with the top in the up position. Have no doubt, Porsche fully intended this car to be used in fair weather. They can, and will, leak. As they age, they begin to take on little drafts, along with wind noise. Without painstaking care, the back window, which is plastic, will scratch and discolor. But, when it's all said and done, nothing beats one of these cars on a 72 degree summer evening that was seemingly created just for driving. One last note on Cabriolets, buyers should always have sellers demonstrate top function. It would be really bad to get your new acquisition home, and find out the top needs $1500 in repairs!

Except for minor exterior changes, these cars remained visually similar from '83 through '89. Picture #50 shows and '89 model Carrera.

Because the overwhelming majority of used 911s (1972-1986) on the market are fitted with the "type 915" transmission, now is a good time to discuss these units. The 915 transmission is a strange mix of super reliable, but incredibly fragile components. Never ever give one of these cars to a valet! I can't tell you how many of these transmissions I have repaired after a valet parking fiasco. One valet, in only one parking episode, can break it, compared to my '81 SC, that is now at 135,000 miles since its first synchro replacement, and still working perfectly.

One can not be in a hurry with these transmissions. The primary techniques to preserve their health and well being are what I call the two-part shift, and a disciplined use of the throttle in first gear. The two-part shift is simply moving the gear lever out of the engaged gear, pausing in neutral, and then engaging the desired gear. For normal everyday driving, up-shifts should be made after reaching a rev-range between 3500 and 4500 rpm. Heavy applications of throttle in first gear will lead to more energetic shifts into second gear, which will certainly lead to premature failure of the second gear synchro assembly.

These cars are not drag racers, and were not built for that type of driving, so please don't do it. Patience really plays an important part in obtaining full life expectancy with these transmissions, especially when they begin to wear.

An early symptom of synchro wear is when one attempts to engage a gear, and the result is a "no-go", pushing against a wall with the flat of your hand feeling. Never attempt to push through this, or you will break that gear, sooner than later. If this symptom occurs, simply move the lever to a different gear, engage it, then move the lever back to the desired gear. More often than not, the lever will slide right in. To avoid having to do this at a traffic light, always slip the transmission back into first gear just before the car stops, and leave the car in gear until the light changes in your favor. Contrary to popular opinion, this will not hurt the clutch, the throw out bearing, or anything else, but just could extend the life of your transmission many thousands of miles. Believe it or not, it will also reduce your stress levels, and as far as I'm concerned, anything that does that is good.

> *Summation:* The 1983 models are the smoothest, most responsive 911SCs of all, although all the SCs are great cars. Engine life is excellent when the car has been correctly driven, brakes are tremendous, and these cars are holding up well cosmetically. The 911SC, all through its six year production run, is a winner!

1984

Carrera! Would you believe it? Another 10! The basic models continue (Coupe, Targa and Cabriolet), but the changes are numerous. The engine has been increased in displacement, for the first time since 1978, from 3.0 to 3.2 liters. "CIS" fuel injection has finally given way to Air Flow Control fuel injection combined with Digital Motor Electronics (DME). Everything concerning DME points toward reliability, but only the long term owner will really know for sure. Horsepower is up to 200 (SAE), compared to 204 for the European 1983 911SC, and the European Carrera puts out an unbelievable 231! For comparison sake, this figure only comes a few horsepower shy of equaling U.S. version 3.0 (1976 and 1977) Turbo Carreras. This car certainly deserves its "Carrera" badge prominently glued to the rear engine lid, just below the air intake grille. That's right, the nameplate has no posts that fit in holes in the lid, it is actually glued to the paint. Oh well, I guess that's progress.

The gray market has taught us something interesting about the cars. A popular option in Europe, but one rarely seen on a car brought in through our Porsche dealer organization, is the use of 7" x 15" diameter front wheels, 8" x 15" diameter rear wheels, high profile (60 series) Dunlop tires, combined with either Boge shocks, or sport suspension that utilizes Bilstein shocks. The wheel and tire combination, when used with Boges, makes for a fabulous car to drive, especially if it is to be used for daily commuting, as well as an occasional romp in the mountains on a Sunday afternoon. I don't understand why more Carreras with this set up have not been ordered by U.S.A. dealers, it is a terrific option. Most showroom cars in the United States dealerships appear with the same sixteen inch diameter wheels and low profile tires that have been extremely popular since 1978.

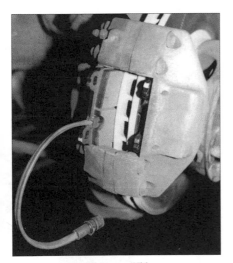

Picture #51

Another change that has appeared with the Carrera is an electrical brake pad wear sensor system (see picture #51). This system is already fitted to 928 and 944 models, but the Carrera is the first 911 to receive it. One brake pad, at each corner of the car, is fitted with a clip-on sensor that, when the pad is sufficiently worn, triggers a warning light on the dashboard. This light does not mean that the car is dangerous to drive, but should be a warning to the car owner that he contact his service facility at the earliest possible convenience. In cases we have seen to date, the brake pads have at least one thousand miles of wear left, once the warning light has been activated, before any additional damage occurs.

Picture #52

Technically a major design change has been incorporated into the Carrera engine. The hydraulic tensioning system for the timing chains has been completely changed (see picture #52). The tensioner no longer relies on its own oil supply, but instead uses engine oil fed into it through special lines (see picture #53 and #54) that attach to the outside of the chain housing cover. These tensioners may be retrofitted to all earlier 911 models, including turbos, and are a solid plus if they have already been installed on an earlier model.

Picture #53

On the luxury side, the Carrera has a welcome feature that no other 911 has ever been fitted with. Electric door locks! Just turn the key in the door lock, and the car is secure. Such a small thing, but oh so nice. We have seen this door lock system incorporated into various alarm systems, when, in response to a remote input, the

Picture #54

system not only disarms the car, it unlocks it for the owner! Very nice, very convenient, very contemporary.

The 3.2 liter cars, built from 1984 through 1989, have developed few problems over the years, but there are some cautions. The first is the engine compartment fuel line, part # 930 110 595 05, that supplies the fuel injectors. This line is a steel section, with three rubber sections branching off of it. The

Picture #55

rubber sections, most often the two that can be seen by looking over the large cooling fan, and then down to the rear of the intake manifold just to the left of the center of the engine, develop heat cracks, and shrinkage (see picture #55). The shrinkage is the most critical, because as the line becomes shorter over time, it starts to pull away from the steel section, allowing seepage to occur. The fix for this requires removal of the intake manifold, replacement of the line, and putting everything back together. Two things should always be done at the same time. 1. Always replace the fuel line, part #930 110 411 99, that you can't see with the manifold in place. This line connects the pressure regulator and pressure damper, and deteriorates over time. 2. Always re-check the fuel mixture following this repair, because the intake manifold has been resealed, and we have seen up to ½% CO change following this job. This repair is not a small ticket item, average cost about $800, so always be sure to inspect the rubber to steel connection points for any sign of seepage or fuel residue.

The second problem is high oil consumption. We have seen this problem on cars ranging in age from 45,000 to 110,000 miles plus, and it is usually attributed to badly worn valve guides. Normal oil consumption for these cars is roughly one quart per 1,000 miles, and we usually recommend a top end (valve) job when consumption approaches one quart per 300 miles. A wide variety of costs can be incurred, from about $2,500 for a straight valve job, to over $8,000, which would

65

include all new valves, new piston/cylinder set, new connecting rod bearings, and all new dilavar cylinder head studs. It's kind of a crap-shoot as to what the engine will need, and it's impossible to give a true estimate until after disassembly. A general rule of thumb is if the car is over 100,000 miles, the rod bearings should be replaced, and the pistons/cylinders should be measured, and replaced if worn past acceptable specification. Our shop always replaces the cylinder head studs, all twenty-four, because we have run across occasional stud failure, in otherwise properly functioning cars. It's not always necessary to replace all the valves, and each engine should be treated on a case by case basis. No more than one or two percent of these cars will need this repair early on, but once they go past 125,000 miles, that percentage figure will go up quickly.

The third problem is brake noise. Asbestos free brake pads have a tendency to become noisy over time, and we have found weekly washing, using a strong stream of water from a garden hose, directed through the wheel openings, helps greatly. Do not do this on anything other than cold wheels, and always drive the car at least two miles in order to dry out the brakes prior to parking the car. Washing will not help the moaning noise, noticeable during slow speed stops, and sometimes during initial movement from rest, that can develop as the miles accumulate. This problem is caused by the brake caliper piston o-rings deteriorating, and becoming sticky. The cure for this is to reseal the front calipers. Please remember also, that the newest 3.2 Carrera is now at least ten years old and they should all have the brake hoses replaced, unless, of course, they have already been done. Caliper reseal cost is approximately $125 for each unit, and brake hose replacement runs about $225, complete.

One additional problem involves the heating system. The control box for the heating system rests between the front seats, and incorporates two levers. When raising these levers, an assist blower in the engine compartment turns on, pushing warmed air forward to the passenger compartment. Each lever also activates an additional blower of its own, and these blowers are hidden behind the carpet in each front foot well. With the ignition switch in the on position each lever should be pulled up individually, and its respective blower should be heard. If a gentle hum occurs on each side of the car, everything is OK. If an objectionable squealing is heard, that foot well blower is bad. If nothing happens, the rear blower may be burned out, both front blowers may be bad, or the electronic control unit for the whole system may have failed. Repairs to this system may be more than $150, and sometimes more than $600.

Summation: The Carrera is going to prove itself as a very special automobile, one that may only have one major flaw. That flaw is going to be the bad reputation that follows the gray market everywhere it goes, and the consumer's ignorance concerning the problems associated with gray market cars. Hopefully not to many of these cars, intended for European use only, found their way, via unscrupulous federalizers, into the United States. Please refer to the chapter of this book entitled "The Gray Market".

1985

The second year of the Carrera is basically the same as the 1984 car, but some interesting changes were made. Electric seats were added, with the right side as an option. There are many variations regarding the electrically operated seats. the least expensive has only up/down controls for the front and rear of the seat bottom, with fore/aft and backrest angle controlled manually. The fully equipped seats have electric controls for all motion adjustment as well as lumbar control

and seat heating. 1985 model seats also sport a slightly different shape, and are extremely comfortable, as well as supportive. See pictures #56 (1971), #57 (Carrera, C2/C4, '85-on), #58 (Carrera sport seat), #59 (cloth covered RS America Sport Seat), and #60 (993)... for some miscellaneous examples of the many different seats/styles Porsche has used.

The windshield washer system has new washer nozzles which are recognizable by their shape. They are wider, longer and flatter than washer

Picture #56

Picture #57

Picture #58

Picture #59   Picture #60

nozzles used on pre-1985 cars, and are electrically heated to avoid freezing in cold climates.

Driveability has been improved with the introduction of a modified shifter system that shortens the "throw" of the shift lever by approximately ten percent, which was accomplished by redesigning linkage components at the lever. Also, an even shorter throw version (we call it the super short shifter) became available as an option. The super short version , known in the Porsche system as option M241, reduces throw a full twenty percent over 1984 and earlier models, but one should be aware that this shifter, really designed for performance driving, has a heavier, stiffer motion, and may not be totally desirable as a result. If the car being purchased is to be used mainly in city and heavy traffic conditions, the super short shifter is definitely not a high priority item.

Summation: A very nicely improved 1984.

1986

Pretty much a replay of the 1985, with a few exceptions. One is a change in the anti-roll bars (also known as sway bars), which have been increased in diameter by 2mm in the front, and 3mm in the rear. This increase, from 20 to 22mm front, and 18 to 21mm rear, make for a more responsive car, because the larger bars reduce body roll, giving the car a more stable feel during rapid cornering. Another benefit is realized during freeway speed lane changes, where recovery after the maneuver is effortless. A negative resulting from this increase in size is that the two rear mounting consoles, that are welded to the chassis, are not strong enough for the bar size increase, and as mileage accumulates, break.

The symptom is a pronounced clunk under the back of the car, noticeable most often while entering or exiting driveways, parking lots, etc., as well as slow speed motion over poor pavement. Repairs of this type should always be done by a welder, or body shop, experienced in chassis repair and metal finishing techniques. The proper procedure is to cut/grind away the original console, and weld in a new, stronger replacement, part # 911 501 983 00 GRV, followed by undercoating to protect the area. We have seen at least a hundred cars with this problem, and the repair should not cost more than $200 per side.

Porsche thought of creature comforts in 1986 as well. The dashboard vent system underwent extensive re-design, and now produces a satisfactory amount of air flow, which also allows the air conditioner to be more effective. Also, the switch knobs for the push/pull switches were reduced in size, along with the cigar lighter knob and the glove box door knob. The new knobs are pleasant visually, but also have an advantage over the old style; now a theft proof removable radio can be removed/replaced without first removing the fog light switch knob and lighter. The 1986 models also have the switch for the rear window defroster moved from above the radio down to the center console, along with the emergency four-way flasher switch, which used to be next to the ignition switch. One "small" item that should not be forgotten concerning the 1986 model year is the reintroduction of the 911 Turbo. Please refer to the "930" chapter for additional information concerning the "new" 911 Turbo.

> *Summation:* The 1986 Carreras are very nice cars that have no serious weaknesses. They are new enough for a buyer to easily find a prime example, even with low mileage, but read on - the 1987s are even better.

1987

A very good car becomes great! Major changes in the drive train create a car that is much easier to deal with in heavy traffic, as well as being totally competent in "sporting" outings. The Carrera Cabriolet, Targa, and Coupe are now fitted with a hydraulic clutch, as well as a totally re-designed transmission that uses a different synchro mechanism. The clutch is wonderfully soft, with a totally predictable release/engagement point, and should wear extremely well. Under ideal circumstances plan on at least 60,000 miles going by between replacements. Speaking of replacement, this clutch is an expensive one, generally costing about $1400 to replace. Add to that another $200 to update the throw out bearing release fork, and the possibility of a flywheel replacement (no surfacing/machining is permitted on the hydraulic clutch flywheels) and the cost has grown to over $2000!

Picture #61

Picture #62

Picture #63

The true beauty of the hydraulic clutch is that it eliminates set up/adjustment errors that are frequently made on 1986 and earlier models, even though the Porsche factory repair manual outlines in detail how to install/adjust clutch cables and related parts. The new synchros in the transmission make driving more pleasant due in whole to the new shifting characteristics they make possible. Through 1986, shifting was done by pushing the lever into the gear one wanted, requiring effort for the entire motion. In contrast, 1987 and later models require a light push of the lever, and the transmission actually feels like it sucks the lever the rest of the way into the desired position. The entire shift requires almost no effort, is extremely smooth, and leaves no doubt as to whether or not the gear being selected has properly engaged. Visually the 1987 models are different from the front, because they are the first U.S. legal cars to be fitted with halogen headlights (see picture #61) that use a replacement bulb, instead of sealed beams (see picture #62) of either incandescent or halogen construction. Incidentally, many 1986 and earlier cars can be seen that are fitted with European Bosch H1 or H4 halogen lamps (see picture #63) although both versions are technically illegal in the States. They

Picture #64

Picture #65

are also different visually from the rear; the large reflector that extends from the left to the right taillight now reads "Porsche" in hologram form (picture #64), rather than the highly visible black letters on earlier models (picture #65). While we're on the subject of lighting, picture #66 depicts the driving (fog) lamps used from 1974 through 1983, and picture #67 shows the driving (fog) lamps used from 1984-1989. The 1987 Turbo, see "930" chapter, aside from the visual differences mentioned above, remains the same as the 1986 models; still outrageous!

Picture #66

Picture #67

Summation: The 1987 Carrera is a wonderfully refined car that is probably the easiest Porsche yet to drive in town or traffic, and is extremely stable on the open road.

1988/1989

What can I say? These cars, although slightly lacking in finish detail quality, compared to 1971 models, are just about perfect. It's too bad that Porsche sold so many Carreras in 1986, and so few in 1989. The 1988 model run included the usual Coupe, Targa, Cabriolet and Turbo line, and a very limited production coupe that was called the Club Sport. This was a very interesting car, one that Porsche put on a diet, deleting the rear seats, power windows, radio, front fog lamps, power seats, air conditioning and a host of other items, ending up with a car that was 155 pounds lighter (plus undercoating-weight unknown) than the basic Carrera Coupe. Combine the weight loss with hollow intake valves, and a special DME unit that allows an additional 320 revs at the top end, and you end up with a car that is 0.2 seconds faster 0-60, and 0.5 seconds faster in the quarter mile than the standard Carrera. This might not sound like much, but the difference in the sound and feel of the car are changed dramatically. Certainly not a car for everyone, but it fills a niche that's been empty for quite some time. Also, on the subject of special edition cars, 1989 has two of its own, one being a silver anniversary model that was the direct opposite of the 1988 Club Sport, being a luxury model rather than a performance model. They were all painted, you guessed it, silver, and had light grey leather interior with a special center console. One interesting option offered within the package was alloy wheels color matched to the exterior color, and most of the cars were ordered that way. The second special 1989 model was the Speedster. Yes, indeed, after being gone for about thirty years, the tiny windshield and goofy top returned, but this time it had Turbo body work, the standard Carrera drive train, most were fitted with air conditioning, and all were an instantaneous success. So much so, that some sold new for forty thousand dollars more than their sticker price! The regular Coupe, Targa and Cabriolet models have created a new expression at our shop; "I never met an '89 I didn't like!". The 1989 cars have very quiet rear view mirrors, inner door handles that have an exceptionally light pulling action, engine management provides extremely smooth acceleration characteristics, obviously due to refined electronics in the DME system, and an overall feeling of high quality pervades. That basically says it all about the 1989 Porsches, except for the Carrera 4, whose story can be found in the chapter titled C2/C4.

Summation: Great cars-no weaknesses!

C2/C4

Probably one of the most spectacular road/performance vehicles ever built to date, but...1989 marked the introduction of the Carrera 4 (the C2s didn't show up until 1990) and it looked like a 911, but changes were numerous! These cars are fitted, as are all C2/C4s through the end of 993 production, with a 3.6 liter engine that is an absolute marvel. Plenty of power and torque allow this car to accelerate all the way through the rev range in a way never seen before in a production 911. Every once in a while, probably too often, that wonderful power had to take these cars back to the dealership, because it's possible that Porsche released this car before its time. Factory information said that this car was approximately 85%

Picture #68

new, which basically meant it was a new model and, perhaps, they got overconfident, due to the immense success of various 911 models built since 1978, and didn't test, test, test. Who knows? I'm not sure, but I do know that many of these cars needed to have the new-look taillight lens' (see picture #68) and rear reflectors replaced because they crack. Porsche had to recall early models, by letter, in March 1991, to have fuel tank sending units replaced. The models affected by this problem were 1989, 1990 and some 1991 C2s and C4s. Another curious problem these cars have is the ash tray. Even if you

don't smoke, you will come back to your parked C2/C4, and the ash tray will be open. "How is this possible?", you might ask. Hopefully, Porsche has figured it out, because the problem has plagued many C2 and C4 cars built at least through the end of 1992. OK, you're about to accuse me of nit-picking, aren't you? Well, I have been, so now we're going

Picture #69

to discuss the serious stuff. If you're looking at a second hand C2/C4, you must check the clutch pedal action. It should be light and smooth, and if it isn't, you must check with a knowledgeable repair facility to see how bad it's going to be. If there is a noticeable clunk when the engine is started, or shut off, it is very likely that the dual mass flywheel is broken. The dual mass flywheel was designed to dampen transmission noises entering the passenger compartment, and it does it well. Unfortunately, when it breaks, the cost of just the part is about $1,150! Add labor and a clutch to that, and you're flirting with a $3,000 repair!

Now things get really serious. If the C2/C4 being looked at was built before approximately June, 1991 (check that VIN plate on the left door jamb for the month/year production date) it must be taken to your very favorite Porsche expert before buying it. An unknown, to me anyway, amount of these cars have oil leaks develop at the joining point between the cylinder heads and cylinders, and when this problem occurs engine disassembly is required. The pistons and cylinders must be replaced, and the cylinder heads must be machined (see picture #70-before, #71-during, and #72-after) to accommodate the new cylinder design, as well as an added head gasket. If this repair is done without assistance from Porsche, it will cost you approximately $6,800. So much for nit-picking! In all fairness to Porsche, they were terrific as far as goodwill repairs were concerned, even in cases where the original warranty had expired for some time, but don't expect any help with these items now.

Now that we have seen many examples of these models go past 50 – 70,000 miles, we are seeing more problems worthy of discussion. These cars leak oil,

Picture #70   Picture #71   Picture #72

and, obviously, some are worse than others. They leak from the crankcase through-bolt o-rings, cylinder base o-rings, chain box covers, oil lines, etc. Even if the car you're interested in buying has no oil spots on the floor where it is regularly parked, the car must be put on a lift, and the under engine noise dampening pan must be removed. Only then can the severity of leakage be correctly evaluated. That tray can trap a lot of oil, and the seller/owner may not even be aware that trouble might be just around the corner. The cost of resealing one of these engines, from the through-bolt o-rings up, is typically about $3,000, and not just anyone can do it. Use extreme care when considering one of these cars, because it can bite you financially. In addition to the engine leakage, there are a few other items to look at. A few inches forward of the right rear wheel, under the trailing edge of the rocker panel, is the thermostat housing that controls oil flow to the front oil cooler. This housing, once it begins to leak, must be replaced with an updated version, as well as new hoses. I won't go into part numbers on this item because the housing has been "improved" a few times already, and my information might be invalid by the time you're reading this. Connecting this housing to the oil source at the oil filter housing is an oil line, part #964 207 254 06, and an additional line between the engine and the filter housing, part #964 207 252 14, that also can leak, and both lines are very expensive to replace. Oil leak related issues can only be diagnosed by an expert Porsche mechanic, so it is crucial that the car in question be looked at by a professional.

One development that Porsche should not feel embarrassed about, that found its way into these cars in the form of an option, is Tiptronic. Finally, an automatic transmission that can be driven in a sporting fashion, or used in the same way you would drive your Taurus. Porsche accomplished this by giving it four speeds, controlled by two selection gates. The left gate is laid out in the traditional automatic format, but once 'D' is selected, the lever may be moved to the right gate, allowing manual upshifting/downshifting by simply "tipping" the lever forward/backward and then allowing the lever to return to the middle position. Each "tip" gives the computer an instruction, which is stored or used immediately, depending on throttle position, rpms, etc. Pages could be written on the intelligence level of this wonderful transmission, because it can do so much, thanks to electronics, but the word "excellent" will have to suffice. This option is available only on the C2, adds about 200 pounds to the car, sacrifices approximately 0.9

second, zero to 60 mph, but can still be driven very, very quickly. If you spend a lot of your time driving in heavy traffic, if you don't like a conventional manual transmission, or if you have a disability that prevents the use of a clutch, but you still like to drive, this option is for you.

Also on the plus side, as I've already stated, the cars are sensational to drive, and just might have the best brakes known to man. The C4, as its name implies, has four wheel drive, with the basic torque split being 31% to the front axle, and 69% to the rear. Both the C2 and C4 are equipped with ABS, airbags, underbody panels that improve aerodynamics, and also make the car quieter from an outside vantage point, as well as wheel housing liners that keep everything nice and tidy under the fenders and quarter panels. The suspension is totally new, using

light alloy control arms on the front, and alloy trailing arms in the rear. Coil springs are used on all four corners, replacing the torsion bars used through the entire 356 and 911 production run, until the C2s and C4s. The rear spoiler is adjustable, automatically raising up into its high speed position at approximately 50 miles per

Picture #73

hour, and then returning to its down setting when the car is slowed to below 10 mph. Porsche has thoughtfully provided a switch in the engine compartment so

Picture #74

the tail may be raised (see picture #73) for cleaning purposes. The wheels are of a new look (see picture #74), which Porsche calls the Club Sport design, or "Design 90" rim, and they are 6" x 16" front, and 8" x 16" rear, but retain the same tire sizes of recent years, which are 205/55 front, and 225/50 rear. Even though it was never considered a problem, the front wheels now have power assisted steering, via a pump driven by the right side camshaft in the engine, and a fluid supply reservoir located in the engine compartment. I would categorize this as an addition one would never hope for, but after driving a C2/C4, and then returning to an earlier model, it is a change that is welcomed. Opinions concerning the C2/C4 styling (please see picture #69) are purely subjective, but my personal observations seem to reveal an approximate even split as to whether it

Picture #75

Picture #76

Picture #77

is liked or disliked, compared to 1989 and earlier Carreras. One change I feel is terrific is the outside rear view mirrors (picture #75), which first appeared on the 1991 Turbo, and then the 1992 C2s and C4s. They are body color, with no trim, are aerodynamic, and absolutely gorgeous.

1993 also witnessed production of a special coupe, the RS America. these models were fitted with a fixed rear spoiler (picture #76), 17" Cup wheels (picture #77), and door panels without

Picture #78

Picture #79

creature comforts (picture #78). The special cloth-covered sport seats were pictured on page 69, picture #59. A/C, sunroof and other items found on most C2s were optional on this car, as well as, surprisingly, limited slip.

The C2/C4 lineup also included two very limited production convertibles. One was built only in 1992, and it was called the America Roadster. These horrendously expensive models were fitted with the same engine and five speed manual transmission as the Carrera 2, but are Turbo bodied Cabriolets. Basically built on the Turbo chassis, they have Turbo brakes, springs, stabilizers (anti-roll bars) and shock absorbers. The standard equipment items include 17" wheels and heated full power seats for both driver and passenger. The other odd-ball convertible was the re-introduction (again) of the Speedster. Like the America Roadster, the Speedster comes standard with 17" wheels, but is fitted with a manually operated top and leather lined bucket seats, and is a narrow bodied car. The door panels are basic, no frill units that do not have armrests or traditional door handles. Also deleted were door storage pockets, power door locks and power mirrors, but the option list was long enough to almost turn one of these cars into a cabriolet with a goofy looking top.

C2/C4 owners must exercise additional care when selecting a technician to maintain their car, because it is not only more complex than earlier models, but the use of System tester 9288 (see picture #79), which is a fault code read-out instrument, must be used at every maintenance interval to be sure all systems in the vehicle are functioning correctly. This tester is extremely expensive, so make sure your mechanic/shop has one in its tool arsenal.

> *Summation:* The C2/C4 line of cars, even with their problems, are arguably the best 911s to date. The handling is superb, the braking capabilities enter into the realm of unbelievable, the fit and finish is good, the A/C really works, and the cars are very fast. Except for the cost per mile bottom line, and their various ills, these cars still must be rated fairly high on the "wow" scale.

270 horsepower! 6-speed transmission! Hydraulic valve adjusters! All new rear suspension! $5,000 price reduction! Porsche is definitely listening. As time goes by, and products are improved, one always has to wonder where it will end. Well, it obviously didn't end with the C2/C4, because the

Picture #80

1995 911 is an absolutely incredible car. It is stunningly beautiful, (picture #80), fast, smooth, quiet, etc., etc. The 6-speed is effortless to operate, the Tiptronic option is still available, the clutch is soft, the power band is very wide, but more exciting over 4,000 rpm, and the brakes are good enough to cause you not only to want to keep track of the distance to the car in front of you, but also keep track of the distance between yourself and the car behind you. Any hurried stop is likely to cause the car to the rear to close at an alarming rate, which should certainly encourage a 993 operator to become a better, more aware driver. "993" has been the term adopted by some people, much as "930" was used when discussing early 911 Turbos, and is simply a project designation number that caught on, and at the time of this writing, seems to be more popular than "1995 911". Changes within the engine of the new car are numerous, the most obvious being the elimination of the need for valve adjustments. This was accomplished by using new rocker arms, cam housings, and various other parts that allow the incorporation of a tiny hydraulic lifter that is part of each rocker arm. Changes were also made to strengthen the crankshaft, and, at the same time, lighten the connecting rods, which results in an overall reduction in weight of the entire crankshaft assembly. The valve train was also lightened, by reducing valve stem diameter by 1.0 millimeter. To go along with all the power, a 17" wheel option (the 993 is fitted with 7/9 X 16" wheels as standard equipment) is available, and the design of both wheel sizes "show off" the huge brake calipers, as well as the cross-drilled rotors.

Keeping the tires clamped tightly to the road is an all new rear suspension system that is an actual subframe that bolts to the body. It is a multi-link design, and uses five control arms (links) at each side, which ensure excellent characteristics, even under heavy loads. Additional changes were also made to the front suspension, all of which increases cornering capability, while, at the same time, makes the car more comfortable to operate in daily conditions. For occupant comfort, the climate control system is now fitted with dust/pollen filters, and the control switches have been re-designed for even more user convenience.

Porsche made their first significant change to the 993 for the model year 1996. It involved a redesign of the intake manifold, is called Varioram (picture #81), and produces a whopping 18% increase in mid-range torque, and the horsepower has been increased to 282.

Picture #81

One somewhat interesting element of the '96 models, coupes only, is that there are documented cases of the rear window exploding. Granted, these mishaps are far and few between, but they have happened. The rear window is a piece of glass complete with the heating wire grid for the defroster installed in the conventional manner. Then a bonding agent is laid along the perimeter of the glass in the form of a bead. The power and ground wires are laid in this bead, and then it hardens to the approximate consistency of a tire sidewall. Then a hard plastic frame, or retainer, that is actually a "U" channel, is laid completely around the outside of the glass, with its own bead of sealant. This frame has three electrical connectors that plug into the car as the assembly is lowered into the body of the car. Once the window is in place, it is glued to the car using a urethane adhesive. Then the decorative molding is snapped on, and the installation is complete.

Rumor has it that two things might happen that cause these windows to explode:

1. Because of body flex, and the window being able to move inside the hard frame, the wiring eventually chafes through the insulation, and as heat builds up, perhaps due to a short, the temper in the glass changes, and it breaks.

2. The other theory is that the dashboard control switch fails to shut off the

circuitry properly, and continuous heat at the window finally affects it to the point where it breaks. Audi had this problem a few years ago, but in this case this is only speculation. Saturn uses a similar technology, but to avoid (1) happening, they have used a more pliable frame, which allows the window to float more, relieving some of the pressure where the wiring is installed.

The only thing here that is certain is that body flex is present, because we have driven many 993s with window squeaks, both front and back. It is obvious that the windows are moving around in these bodies, which must be a contributing factor to rear windows exploding. I have not been able to obtain any official answers from anyone in the Porsche system, nor have I been able to find any technical bulletins regarding this situation, so, for now, we can only hope the problem is so rare that we'll never experience it.

'96 also saw the re-introduction of the Turbo (pictures #82, 83 and 84), this

Picture #82

time in twin turbo configuration. In case you don't know, not much more needs to be said than 400 horsepower, and 400 lb/ft of torque! Oh my! Only the most phenomenal car ever built, by anyone, anywhere, at any time. Everything the older turbo had is better, much better, in the new car.

Picture #83

Picture #84

Picture #85

Picture #86

Unbelievable acceleration and braking, superb handling, beautiful fit and finish, like all 993s, etc., etc., etc.

1996 also saw the introduction of another new model, maybe my all time favorite, the C4S (see the Arena Red beauty on the front cover). This car has the Turbo's bodywork, 18" wheels, the huge red turbo brakes, and is fitted with the basic 993 engine, and the 6 speed manual transmission. The rear spoiler is the pop-up type, not the turbo "whale-tail", which gives the car a muscular, but somewhat elegant, look. The car has four wheel drive, as does its little brother, the C4, which was also re-introduced in '96. The C4 is basically a regular 993, with four wheel drive and the six speed manual transmission. The Tiptronic option is only available on two wheel drive models in coupe, Targa and Cabriolet form. Targa? I'll get to that in a minute. There is a visual difference, seen from the rear, regarding '95 models, compared to '96 and later coupes. The third brake light, or high mount brake light, what we call a basket handle (picture #85), is mounted on the upper edge of the rear engine lid on '95s. For '96 and later, this light was moved up to the top of the rear window (picture #86), and blends in with the roofline.

Picture #87

Porsche re-invented the Targa (picture #87), by throwing out the old design, and starting with a clean sheet of paper. The new Targa has a glass panel that serves as the roof, and when opened, slides back, and under, the rear window. This leaves a huge opening for fresh air to enter, and the top can be opened or closed while the car is moving. Moving on to the '97 models, very little was changed, but another new model was added, the Carrera S. This car has the basic 993 drive train, including suspension and brakes, but is fitted with turbo body work, including what appears to be a split rear spoiler of the pop-up type, none of which produces a performance advantage, just a more aggressive styling approach. And, finally, Porsche has illuminated the ignition switch, after all these years, with a little shine down light tied into the interior light circuit. Will wonders never cease.

> *Summation:* If the 993s continue to prove themselves to be reliable cars, and it certainly looks good so far, they will certainly be the best 911s ever.

The Gray Market

Much has been said about importation of European model Porsches, that are not required to meet emission and safety standards similar to those U.S. models are required to meet. Euro model 911s are easy to spot, because even when converted they almost always have their fender mounted (see picture #85) turn signals still intact.

Basically, the problems that involve the gray market cars are mechanic-created. I really shouldn't use the term "mechanic", it is much too nice, as well as professional, a term to describe most people that perform these conversions. The problems we have seen, on at least 90% of gray market cars, have been aesthetic, electrical, and mechanical. The aesthetic atrocities range from extremely poor welding on exhaust components, such as cat-

Picture #85

alytic converters and exhaust gas recirculation systems, to placement of charcoal canisters (hung by hose clamps in the engine compartment, or front trunk compartment), improper routing of canister hoses, poor hardware to secure collision protection door beams, etc.

The catalytic converter supplied by Porsche works well on a proper conversion, but because of its cost we have seen everything from aftermarket converters (that were so large the lower left valve cover could not be removed) to Volvo converters (two of them welded together) to unidentifiable units welded on to these cars. There are two primary disadvantages to not using a Porsche converter. One, there is not a provision for checking exhaust emissions before the catalyst, a procedure that is necessary at all tune-ups, in order to properly set the fuel injection, and if there is no access plug this critical check cannot be made. Two, all cars built by Porsche for sale in the United States, since mid 1978, have a heat shield covering the catalytic converter. This heat shield protects the inner sidewall of the left rear tire, and to date we have not seen one gray market car fitted with a heat shield on a non-Porsche converter equipped car.

The charcoal canister is a container filled with activated charcoal that traps hydrocarbon fumes. These fumes are then purged by fresh air from the engine cooling fan, and forced to mix with intake air at the air filter housing. This insures a recirculation and containment of fumes that would ordinarily enter the atmosphere. This canister, when supplied by Porsche, has a beautiful little mounting bracket, and a carefully chosen place for its location (under the right quarter panel, forward of the wheel). The canister hoses are routed through specific areas to avoid problems during maintenance and repair operations, and even though all the fittings, tubes and holes for these hoses are in all cars, we have seen conversion shops tie-rap these hoses to cooler pipes, air conditioning hoses, horns, transmission mounts, spark plug wires, and just about everything else in the car. Also, the canister itself might be in the engine compartment (usually in the way of service technicians), in the trunk (usually in the way of the owner), or just tied to something under the car (aesthetically incorrect).

Door beams are steel units designed to improve structural integrity of the doors in order to increase occupant protection in the event of a collision. They are standard equipment on all cars sold in the United States by Porsche, but have to be added to vehicles brought in for conversion. These units are bolt in, to avoid paint damage during welding, and the hardware used to do this operation, in some cases, is terrible, and easily visible when the door is opened. Also, we have seen door beams that rattle because of their construction. This complicates the problem because this situation can be very tricky to repair.

Electrical problems involve the fuel management system that is incorporated into the fuel injection to help the vehicle to run clean enough to satisfy our clean air requirements. These problems manifest themselves in a myriad of ways, most often involving poor cold start symptoms, surging, poor deceleration characteristics, and poor throttle response. This all adds up to a car that can be quite unpleasant to drive.

Other electrical problems are generally ones that involve lights. If the conversion facility did the job right, although they rarely do, they would have purchased all new United States legal light housings and installed them. This is expensive, so their answer to the problem is to add bulbs and bulb holders of inferior quality, glue red plastic under amber lenses, twist bare ends of wires together, and an assortment of sins there is absolutely no excuse for.

Mechanical problems usually go hand in hand with the aesthetic ones, involving cheap, aftermarket parts that are installed in a manner where they interfere with repair or maintenance procedures. The 911 automobile is so unbelievably well laid out that we have become spoiled, but still there is no reason for a charcoal canister to be mounted in the spark plug access area, or the catalytic converter to be such that it has to be removed in order to adjust the valves.

Our shop had the opportunity to perform the Environmental Protection Agency (EPA) and Department of Transportation (DOT) conversion on a new 1985 911 Carrera in February, 1985. We had no financial limitations (and would not have accepted the job had there been any) so we used all Porsche parts, except for fuel management modifications. The catalytic converter, heat shield, charcoal canister, light assemblies, fuel tank filler neck, decals, and all other changes necessary, duplicated an automobile built by Porsche for sale in the United States. The fuel management system incorporated a factory control box modified by a local specialist, which essentially converted it to a U.S. legal unit. The car passed all tests on the first try, runs as smoothly as any factory prepared car, has good throttle response, and is aesthetically pure. Presently, the car is being used daily, follow up checks have revealed no difficulties of any type, and the owner is satisfied with the certification cost. We are not in the gray market business, but this conversion could have been performed for six thousand dollars, providing a nice profit for the conversion facility, and a beautiful car for the consumer.

Summation: Once we proved to ourselves that a gray market 911 could be converted with Porsche level quality and parts, we have become more and more disgusted with every new Carrera or Turbo we see that has been hacked up without mercy in the sole pursuit of the almighty greenback. There have to be fewer quality people, and Porsche purists, in the gray market we have been exposed to, than in any other phase of the industry. If you are looking for a gray market car, be extra careful that the beauty goes further than skin deep. This car will cost you a lot of money, and when you add the price of problem correction to the purchase price, you might be better off consulting the classified ads in search of a similar, but made for the U.S.A. model.

Technical Specs

Year	Model	Bore x Stroke	Disp. in liters	Intake Valve/Port		Exhaust Valve/Port		Comp. Ratio	Fuel System	DIN HP/RPM	Torque/RPM
65-67	911	80 x 66	2	39	32	35	32	9.0:1	Solex Carbs.	130/6100	128/4200
									Weber Carbs.	130/6100	128/4200
67	911S	80 x 66	2	42	36	38	35	9.8:1	Weber Carbs.	160/6600	132/5200
68	911/911L	80 x 66	2	39	32	35	32	9.0:1	Weber Carbs.	130/6100	128/4200
69	911T	80 x 66	2	42	32	38	32	8.6:1	Weber Carbs.	110/5800	116/4200
69	911E	80 x 66	2	42	32	38	32	9.1:1	Mech. Inj.	140/6500	129/4500
69	911S	80 x 66	2	45	36	39	35	9.8:1	Mech. Inj.	170/6500	134/5500
70-71	911T	84 x 66	2.2	46	32	40	32	8.6:1	Zenith Carbs.	125/5800	130/4200
70-71	911E	84 x 66	2.2	46	32	40	32	9.1:1	Mech. Inj.	155/6200	141/4500
70-71	911S	84 x 66	2.2	46	36	40	35	9.8:1	Mech. Inj.	180/6500	147/5200
72-73	911T	84 x 70.4	2.4	46	32	40	32	7.5:1	Mech. Inj.	140/5600	148/4000
72-73	911E	84 x 70.4	2.4	46	32	40	32	8.0:1	Mech. Inj.	165/6200	152/4500
72-73	911S	84 x 70.4	2.4	46	36	40	36	8.5:1	Mech. Inj.	190/6500	159/5200
73 1/2	911T	84 x 70.4	2.4	46	30	40	33	8.0:1	CIS Inj.	140/5700	148/4000
74	911	90 x 70.4	2.7	46	32	40	32	8.0:1	CIS Inj.	150/5700	175/3800
74	911S	90 x 70.4	2.7	46	35	40	35	8.5:1	CIS Inj.	175/5800	187/4000
74	Carrera	90 x 70.4	2.7	46	35	40	35	8.5:1	CIS Inj.	175/5800	187/4000
75	911S	90 x 70.4	2.7	46	35	40	35	8.5:1	CIS Inj.	175/5800	175/4000
75	Carrera	90 x 70.4	2.7	46	35	40	35	8.5:1	CIS Inj.	175/5800	175/4000
76-77	911S	90 x 70.4	2.7	46	35	40	35	8.5:1	CIS Inj.	165/5800	176/4000
76-77	Turbo	95 x 70.4	3	49	32	41.5	36	6.5:1	CIS Inj.	245/5500	253/4000
78-79	911SC	95 x 70.4	3	49	39	41.5	35	8.5:1	CIS Inj.	180/5500	175/4200
78-79	Turbo	97 x 74.4	3.3	49	32	41.5	34	7.0:1	CIS Inj.	265/5500	291/4000
80-83	911SC	95 x 70.4	3	49	34	41.5	35	9.3:1	Motronic Inj.	207/5900	192/4800
84-89	Carrera	95 x 74.4	3.2	49	40	41.5	38	9.5:1	Motronic Inj.	217/5900	195/4800
86-89	Turbo	97 x 74.4	3.3	49	32	41.5	34	7.0:1	CIS Inj.	282/5500	287/4000
90-94	C2/C4	100 x 76.4	3.6	49	41.5	42.5	38	11.3:1	Motronic Inj.	247/6100	228/4800
91-92	Turbo	97 x 74.4	3.3	49	32	41.5	34	7.0:1	CIS Inj.	315/5750	332/4500
93-94	Turbo	100 x x76.4	3.6	49	41.5	42.5	38	7.5:1	CIS Inj.	355/5500	383/4500
95	993	100 x 76.4	3.6	49	43.5	42.5	38	11.3:1	Motronic Inj.	270/6100	247/5000
96-98	993	100 x 76.4	3.6	49	43.5	42.5	38	11.3:1	Motronic Inj.	282/6100	250/5250
96-97	Turbo	100 x 76.4	3.6	49	41.5	42.5	38	8.0:1	Motronic Inj.	400/5850	400/4500

This Spec. Page Covers USA Legal Models-For Further Info Use Other Sources

The Airbox

The airbox is one item on the 911 automobile, beginning with the 1973½ 911T, and ending with the 1983 911SC, that is going to leave you stranded.

Sooner or later it is going to get you! It is black plastic, molded in two major sections that are fastened together, using both epoxy and screws, and provides a mounting surface for the air filter and filter housing, the intake air throttle body, the sensor plate housing and fuel distributor, the cold start injector, and various switches and controls that perform as integral components of the fuel injection system. It also provides the central chamber of the intake manifold, allowing attachment of the intake air pipes that deliver a precise flow of air to the intake ports of the cylinder heads. The airbox basically just goes along for the ride, until one day when the car is started, an explosion, which is the airbox blowing up, is heard from the rear of the car. This noise can vary in intensity from a muffled firecracker to a cherry bomb, and is usually accompanied by a small amount of white smoke whisping from the intake air grille of the engine lid. Chance of fire on the initial bang is minimal, but if an attempt is made to start the car after damage is done, there is a great risk of fire. This is because the cold start injector is likely to spray fuel onto the top of the engine, which usually has a liberal coating of grease, oil and dirt on it, and this mixture only needs one spark to cause major problems. When the airbox blows, call a tow truck, do not try to start the car!

This chart will provide information compiled by our shop, during the last few years, concerning airboxes.

During the repair (replacement) of a blown air box, there are certain items that should be attended to. The most important element of every air box job is cleanliness. To avoid air leaks, injection system contamination, and other problems, the top of the engine has to be cleaned thoroughly, all gasket surfaces have to be prepared properly, and all open fuel lines have to be kept plugged to prevent entry of debris. After the blown air box has been removed, and the top of the engine is exposed, there are three parts that should always be replaced during cleanup. The crankcase breather hose (part number 901 107 394 00 through 1979, and part number 930 107 394 10 for 1980 through 1983 models) becomes hard and brittle, and will leak when reinstalled. The oil pressure switch (part number 911 606 230 00) for the dashboard warning light probably is already leaking, and the oil thermostat o-ring (part number 999 707 172 40) will surely

Diagram 24

Year Model	Porsche Part Number	Avg. Life Expectancy of Original Airbox	Engine Removal Required?
'73½	911 110 140 00	30,000 mi.	no
'74-'77	911 110 904 00	40-60,000 mi.	no ('74-'75), yes ('76-'77)
'78-'79	911 110 906 00	50-70,000 mi.	yes
'80	911 110 904 00	50-70,000 mi.	yes
'81-'83	911 110 904 00	80-120,000 mi.	yes

begin to leak before engine removal is again required. All three of these items are very difficult to replace with the engine in the car, and the fuel injection system in place, but require a grand total of thirty minutes to do while an airbox is being replaced.

On models that engine removal is required for the necessary repairs, there is one additional item that should always be taken care of prior to reinstallation. The transmission mainshaft seal is now made from an improved material, and should always be replaced in order to insure maximum protection for the clutch from transmission oil contamination. The part number for the improved seal is 999 113 283 40, and every quality shop should have this part in stock. It only takes a few minutes to replace, and could add an additional 30,000 miles of life to the clutch, allowing it to wear out naturally, rather than failing from oil saturation.

Incidentally, I'm sure you have noticed that the average life expectancy figure, in diagram 24 above, for '81 to '83 models, is considerably higher than the earlier models. This is because of an extremely nice modification done by the factory that involves the fuel being injected into the engine during cold starting. On earlier models fuel is simply sprayed into the central chamber of the airbox, from the cold start injector, and then pulled into the engine via manifold vacuum. The improved airbox has a diffuser built into the central chamber that allows fuel from the cold start injector to be injected directly into each of the six intake manifold pipes. This eliminates a build up of fuel vapor in the airbox itself, and instantly increases airbox life dramatically. The factory even did something nice for us so we could identify the improved airbox by a quick visual check. On early airboxes the small screws holding the upper and lower halves of the box together are slotted for installation using a flat bladed screw driver, and the improved boxes are fastened with Phillips head screws. These screws can be found around the left side perimeter of the box, or underneath the air filter insert, which can be removed by loosening the two heavy rubber straps on the air filter cover, and lifting the cover, together with filter, up and back from the engine. Additionally, all new replacement airboxes from Porsche, except for the box used on the 1973½ T, have been updated, and are being manufactured with this internal improvement. Therefore, it is entirely possible to purchase a 1976 911S that has already had an improved air box installed, which would be a very nice plus to consider.

> *Summation:* To obtain maximum life from the airbox, starting procedures for each model, which are outlined in the owners manual found in the glovebox, should be adhered to exactly. Another important factor is to follow the maintenance schedule, as it is outlined in the owners manual, in order to keep the car in a proper state of tune. But, even with all the precautions mentioned, it's still going to get you!

The Engine: Rebuilt or Patched?

I'm sure a lot of you have wondered exactly what takes place during the overhaul of your Porsche's engine. Obviously, it's removed from the car, placed on an engine stand, and "torn down" using an array of impact wrenches, pliers, and screwdrivers. Gasp! Impact wrenches? If your guy takes your 911 engine apart with power tools, you will have to keep a very close eye on him indeed. See what I mean? You really don't know what takes place, so this chapter is actually about what should take place, rather than just what takes place. With the engine on the stand, the exhaust system, induction system, sheet metal, alternator and wire looms are removed, and placed out of the way. Then the real work starts. During disassembly hand tools must be used. Impact wrenches are to fast, and do not allow enough time for the technician to look at things, or think. Looking and thinking are the two most important phases of the project, so why cut either short? Disassembly involves much more than unscrewing things. All major parts, from the ignition distributor to the intermediate shaft, should be scrutinized, so the technician already begins to get a feel for this, your, engine. This inspection during teardown tells a story, and this story, if read correctly, will help make it possible for your rebuilt engine to live a long, happy life.

Before I forget, let's go back to your car for a moment, and glance into the empty engine compartment. Are the fuel line connections plugged with clean plastic, or rubber, line caps? Is the bell housing tied up to the shock towers so the transmission sits at an angle close to which it is at with the engine installed? Tie up the trans? Sure, because if you don't, the center tunnel of your car will probably be full of transmission oil shortly after you get to drive it again. When the trans is allowed to hang free, pressure is applied to, and damages, the shift fork seal at the end of the trans you can't see. When the engine is put back in, the trans becomes level again, and, as the car is shifted oil seeps past the damaged seal. Trans oil stinks, and if you have ever gotten into a car with a contaminated center tunnel that's been parked in the hot sun for four hours, you will definitely want to check to see if your trans is tied up.

Back to the engine stand. Rocker arms are the first parts that require special treatment during removal. They are each held in place by rocker arm shafts, one per arm, in an aluminum housing, called the cam housing (picture #86), with precision bores that accept these shafts. These bores, during the engine's lifetime, become dirty, and must be cleaned prior to shaft removal, or the dirt will be trapped, and scratch the aluminum, and these scratches can allow leakage after the engine is put back together. Amazing, fifteen minutes of cleaning during disassembly eliminates an unbelievably irritating leak in the finished product. The rocker arms themselves have a precision machined surface that contacts, metal to metal, the lobe of the camshaft that operates it. This contact has been a long and wearing relationship, and must be kept intact. As each rocker is removed, it should be placed on a tray that is pre- labeled with "intake-cyl #1", etc. This

Picture #86

insures no mixups until it is known whether or not the camshafts are reusable. The same is done with pistons and cylinders, they must be numbered during removal, even though they are almost never reused.

Once disassembly is complete, including cleaning and assessment of the cylinder heads, engine case, and crankshaft/connecting rod assembly, you may lose track of your project. More often than not, your technician does not have the capability to perform machine work related refurbishment of critical components, and must rely on an outside shop to perform these tasks. This is certainly OK, as long as he has a working knowledge of the machine processes, so he can critique the machinists work prior to assembly.

Engine cases usually require unique repairs, the most common is installation

Picture #87

of some type of threaded insert (see picture #87) into each cylinder head stud hole. Normally, this repair is done to magnesium alloy cases, manufactured from 1968 through 1977, that are to be used in performance applications, displacement and compression increases, have had prior repairs, and in all cases during repair of any 2.7 liter engine. There are

93

probably far more ways to do this wrong than right. One is to, after stud removal, of course, place the case on the work bench, drill out the existing threaded holes to the size required using a hand drill, installing timeserts, helical coils, or threaded sleeves (case savers), and putting the studs back. This method creates grief! There is no way to get the studs consistently perpendicular to the case, which means your technician will need a huge hammer to get the cylinders, and then the heads, down over these studs that now point about every way except where they are supposed to. If he's able to get this done, and then get the heads torqued, just think about those bent studs with all those loads, all those temperature changes...

Picture #88

Picture #89

A preferred method of case saver installation is to place half of the case in a mill fixture, drill and tap out the holes, install the steel sleeves using red "Loctite", flycutting (see picture #88 and #89) the cylinder base surfaces to insure perfect seating, rebore the cylinder spigots to insure a good cylinder fit (see picture #90), and then replace the studs, which will be perfectly straight, just like they were prior to the repair. Whether your techni-

Picture #90

cian or his machinist performs this repair, it is critical for long engine life. As far as the studs are concerned, many opinions have been offered. A good rule of thumb is if the originals are in good condition, and the engine will be stock, or have minor modifications, use them again. If a massive amount of horsepower is the goal, use Dilavar studs, and if the studs are rusty replace them, also using Dilavar units. If early studs are mixed with Dilavar studs, use all early types on top (intake side), and all Dilavars on the bottom (exhaust side).

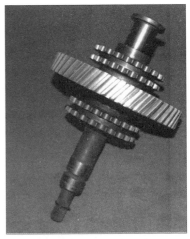

Picture #91

Are we done with the case yet? Nope. Now the mating surfaces must be cleaned, all high spots removed with a surface plate and fine emery paper, and the two halves assembled with no internal pieces in place. This allows the technician to measure the crankshaft main bearing bore (picture #92) to determine if it is true, or has to be cut to alleviate side pressure against the crank after final assembly. This bore is originally cut with a reamer, so what better way to either cut it back to original size, or cut it to first oversize (+ .25mm)? Having a reamer means your technician or his machinist has made a heck of a financial investment, and is very serious about his work. If your engine has an aluminum case, don't be fooled and skip this part of the job. Although the frequency that line bore will be required is far less than it is with magnesium cases, it still must be verified as OK. Now the case is done, except for final cleaning and assembly preparation.

The crankshaft has gears on one end. The brass one turns the ignition distributor

Picture #92

and the steel one turns the aluminum gear of the intermediate shaft (picture #91), which in turn drives both camshafts using chains, and the oil pump using a splined shaft. Once again, metal to metal wear must be looked at extra carefully, with the result almost always being replacement of the intermediate shaft and its drive gear on the crank. Excessive wear occurs in the root areas of the big aluminum gear, which in turn creates a cyclic grinding noise that you won't want your nice new engine to make. If the steel gear on the crank looks good, but the shaft gear is worn, your technician may elect to just replace the shaft, but there is always a small element of risk involved in this decision. Timing chains always get replaced, but chain wheels and sprockets are low wear items, and each should be inspected and replaced, or reused, as your technician sees fit. Note that the intermediate shaft, when replaced, comes complete with two new chain drive sprockets, so doubt concerning these units is eliminated automatically. Down the shaft resides the oil pump. One bulletproof oil pump. Not a lot has to be done with it, except to make sure it turns smoothly, and doesn't have any chipped teeth. If it's disassembled, care must be taken to keep all the gears in order, and put them back exactly the same as they were. Once all this gear and sprocket and chain stuff is taken care of, the crankshaft can be magnafluxed (crack checked). This should be done with the gears off, and almost always has to be done outside the repair facility. The only precaution here is to record the number of the crank before sending it out, and making sure the same crank comes back. Next, each bearing journal must be measured, polished and remeasured. Most shops can do this, and the only requirement is a good micrometer, a factory manual, and a crank polisher. Polishing may be done on a lathe, but experience and care are mandatory to do it correctly. Final cleaning can be done with a clean, oil based solvent, and pipe stem brushes, which are great to scrub the oil passages with. The crank is now ready for gear installation, done by heating the gears in an oil bath, and quickly pushing them into place. Now the rods may be installed, if they are done, that is.

Connecting rods, also known as con rods, or just rods, bolt to the crankshaft

using two bolts and two nuts each (picture #93). These bolts and nuts are only designed for use once, and must be replaced if they are torqued, and then loosened. Obviously, don't use new hardware to recondition the rods, always use the old stuff. The reconditioning phase of the rods is extremely intricate. Even some machine shops don't do it, but elect to have a rod rebuilder do them.

Picture #93

96

Again, your technician must be knowledgeable enough to determine the quality level of this repair, and once he has them in hand, and has ascertained that the crankshaft end is the correct size and the bushing at the other end is installed and pin fit correctly, he may install them with new bearings and hardware. A light film of lubrication, half STP and half 30W oil is good for this purpose, should be applied to the bearing half shells at the time of assembly. The six rods may be put on the crank in any order, but each rod is numbered, and has a matching rod cap that is stamped with the same number. Torque specs, as in all other applications, should be adhered to exactly as outlined in Porsche repair manuals.

WOW! The bottom end is assembled, all the extra silicone sealant has been carefully wiped away from the mating surfaces of the crankcase halves.... Wait a minute! Silicone? Take it back apart and try again. Silicone sealants (see picture #94 and #95) have a habit of turning into little rubbery balls that can circulate through the engine, looking for a tiny lubrication orifice to plug up, causing component failure somewhere far from home, on a rainy night, at three in the morning. Oh, I forgot, you don't drive your car in the rain, but you get the point. For assembly of magnesium engine cases use a product like Curil K2. Your technician better know how to obtain it, as well as Loctite 574 for aluminum crankcase assembly, as well as camshaft housing to cylinder head assembly. Now, finally, the bottom end really is together. All the silicone has been wiped away, surfaces have been re-cleaned with lacquer thinner and

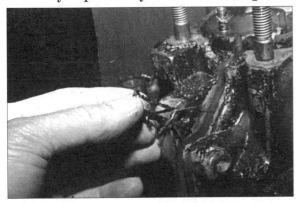

Picture #94

Picture #95

Q-tips, proper sealant has been applied, and viola!

Pistons, big money. Let's skip these and go to the cylinder heads first. Once again, required ingredients: Knowledge, talent, experience and tooling. Lapping valves and putting the head together was OK for your Ford Model A, or your 36 HP VW, but 911 heads are a different animal. The valve seats have to be ground to three different angles, with each cut having to be within a certain margin. If the seat is cut too deeply it has to be replaced, which requires a precision vertical mill and lots of experience. Before the seats are even looked at, the valve guides have to be replaced. This operation takes place after the heads, six per engine, have been degreased and glass bead blasted. Then the heads are heated to about 400 degrees, so the old guides may be removed without damage to the aluminum of the cylinder head. Here is the big, big secret. Allow the heads to cool to room temperature, and measure every valve guide bore, calculate installation press, and machine a new guide for every bore. Then, the heads have to be reheated, so the new guides can safely be installed without any aluminum damage. Now everything has to cool down again. The next step is to ream each guide to the proper dimension, and finally, grind the seats, Once that's done, all the old valves have to be measured and evaluated, and replaced as necessary. The new valves should be placed in the grinder for a final check on the seating surface and then put in the lathe for a final polish on the stem. Overkill. Perfect engines all have a degree of overkill built in. Big, big secret number two. The valve seats in your heads have been ground, right? That means that the valve now sticks out the other side of the head further, right? Right. Now the valve stems have to be ground in order to retain correct valve train geometry, an absolute must for proper performance. Once that is done the valve springs are installed, according to specifications found in Porsche technical manuals. Of course, before final assembly takes place, each of the six matching heads from an engine have to be placed in a vertical mill, or lathe, and be resurfaced if necessary. Only a qualified machinist or master mechanic with machinist training, should be allowed to perform this task.

OK, back to the pistons and cylinders. There is a copper shim/gasket that fits between the base of the cylinder and the engine case. On crankcases that have received case savers this is the surface that was flycut after the inserts were installed. If the flycut was done material that used to be there isn't there any more. If the cylinder heads had to be resurfaced, material is missing there also. All these measurements are important because the combination of the cylinder base shim and the amount of material removed from the surfaces mentioned determines the final clearance between the piston and combustion chamber of the cylinder head. I know, now it's starting to get confusing. But this is when a so-so engine becomes a great engine. For example, if the original engine had about .065" clearance between the piston and head at the tightest point, with the original .010" thick base shim in place, and .008" was removed from the case, and .003" was removed from the heads, that means your technician is now dealing with .054" clearance using the .010" base shims included in the factory engine gasket set. To re-establish the original clearance, a thicker shim must be used, and they are available for this purpose. Instead of "stacking" two .010" shims under each cylinder, one .020" shim should be used. Your technician should know what a good plus/minus factor for the final clearance is, and this clearance should always be measured before assembly. This takes lots of time, but pays big dividends when the engine is finished. To do the measurement, a piston must be installed on a rod, and then a cylinder placed over the piston. At this point something crushable, such as .090" hollow core solder, should be glued to the piston dome at a point that comes closest to the combustion chamber, your technician should know where, and the crankshaft should be rotated slightly off of top dead center. An ideal adhesive is 3M yellow weatherstrip glue, it is good enough to hold the solder, but easy to clean after the measurement. Now install a cylinder head and torque it using all four nuts. Rotate the crankshaft slowly in the direction that will bring the piston all the way to the end of its stroke, so the solder will actually be squashed between the piston and cylinder head. Obviously, if something to hard, that's crushable, is used, damage is possible, so this action must be done very slowly with no force. Once the piston is fully extended, and has done its crushing, it will begin its return stroke. At this point remove the head, dislodge the solder, or clay, or silly putty, etc. and measure the crushed portion with a micrometer. You now have your piston clearance verified, and if correction is necessary, do it with different cylinder shims. With this done, all the pistons, cylinders, cylinder heads and camshaft housings may be installed. This is the fun part, because that tiny lower end has just blossomed into something big, something that is actually starting to resemble an engine. Once the heads and cam housings

99

are torqued...Whoops! We have to back up again. Make sure no sealant of any kind is used on those cylinder base shims. They are designed to be installed dry, and must be put on dry. Also, much has been said about cylinder wall lubrication during the assembly process. If you want the rings to seat properly, in a short amount of time, without massive quantities of exhaust smoke, put them on dry with just a light film of oil on the rings. Do not soak the assembly, or use any form of STP type lubricant on the cylinder walls, or your rings may never seat.

Picture #96

Now is a great time to do something that is almost never done. There are two chain housings, also known as chain cases or chain boxes (see picture #96), that are part of the 911 engine. These housings have press fit pins (see picture #97) that hold the chain tensioners in place. It is not uncommon to see these pins start to come loose, especially in the early magnesium housings used until mid year production of the 1977 cars. If the pin is loose, the case is a throw-away. The replacement will be aluminum, and will seal correctly against either magnesium or aluminum crankcases. From the chain case to completion of the project there will be no need for any type of sealant use. All current technology gaskets are made to be put on dry, and all the o-rings require is a light film of oil. Getting back to the chain case pins, if they are tight that is, you will notice that some sort of epoxy was placed on the backside of each box (see picture #98) where these pins are mounted. This epoxy should be carefully cleaned away, and then re-applied. The best product for this purpose is "Loctite" Loc-

Picture #97

Picture #98

Weld, which is a cold bonding compound packaged in two tubes, and mixed together as needed. This mixture should also be put on the chain guide mounting pins, and all the oil galley plugs on the engine case. Just another nice touch that helps produce that special engine.

OK, time to look at those camshafts (picture #99). The lobes are the areas that contact the faces of the rocker arms. These lobes may have dull gray markings, and some shiny areas, but no pitting is permissible. If they are pitted, they're junk. The faces of the rocker arms should be the same, no low spots, no pitting, just a smooth machine arc.

Damaged rocker arms are sometimes rebuildable, which requires installation of a new

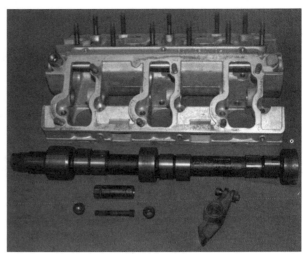

Picture #99

bushing and resurfacing the face. The decision is strictly up to your technician/machinist, because every engine has unique situations in this area. The rocker arm shafts, that were so carefully removed without scratching the cam housings, also have to be examined. These shafts may be reused, but should be measured and polished. You'll notice that only one side of each shaft shows wear, so during installation turn them so the good side is toward the loaded side of the rocker arm bushing, provided they measure within specifications.

After the cam housings are torqued, using the procedure outlined in the Porsche technical manual, the chain housings are installed. Remember, do not use any sealant on those gaskets. I know it's tempting, but don't. Chain guides, chain wheels, chain wheel shims and end plates, and the tensioners all can be installed. Shims? Doesn't "shims" usually mean something has been set up? Sure does. Back to the big Porsche book! Was one or both of your cams replaced, or were the shims mixed up during removal? In the case of a yes answer, the procedure is outlined for sprocket depth measurement, which insures that the chain wheels at the cams will be in perfect alignment with the drive sprockets on the intermediate shaft. Your technician will need a precision straight edge and a very good depth caliper, because these measurements must be accurate.

Now that we've gotten to this point, you have to understand, in order to keep this chapter shorter than "Excellence was Expected", ensuing procedures for camshaft timing, and rocker shaft/rocker arm installation has to be done strictly as outlined in the Porsche manual. Your technician should know this procedure intimately, with one possible exception. The rocker shafts should be clean and dry for the installation procedure. Do not oil them, or chances are very good that they will leak. After all the rocker arms, and shafts, are installed, torqued, and adjusted, the engine should be turned through at least ten crankshaft revolutions, all the rocker arms readjusted, and just prior to valve cover installation, a liberal amount of oil should be applied to the rockers, being careful to introduce oil to the lubrication holes in each rocker arm.

Well, I guess all that's left is to put the fuel and exhaust systems back on, after a careful cleaning and inspection, of course, and then installation of the complete unit. If all torque specifications were adhered to, and all procedures were followed as outlined in the Porsche manual, all you have left to do is charge the battery, start the engine, set the dwell, (when applicable) and timing, and the fuel mixture, and go for a drive. WOW!

The Aftermarket

One of the hardest things to do concerning Porsches is to convince an owner that aftermarket accessories and mechanical add-ons are not very good. Maybe these pieces are good enough to do what their manufacturer claims they do, but rarely do they do it well. I'm not talking about floor mats here, I'm talking about anti-roll bar kits, airbox pop off valves, reproduction wheels, rebuilt clutch assemblies, short shift kits, and a host of other items not produced for, and quality control checked by, Porsche. We see these items, that someone has installed during a particular car's life, frequently, and they never seem to work out. Anti-roll bars are nice, but they are almost always noisy because their locating bushings are generally plastic, instead of rubber, as originally used by Porsche. Of course, the plastic bushings serve a purpose, they control the movement of the bar precisely, because the harder bushings eliminate almost all movement under heavy loads. Too bad they creak, squeak and groan continuously under light loads and slow speeds.

Airbox pop off valves, designed to prevent airboxes from blowing, have been on the market for a while now, and already are responsible for a few "emergencies" at our facility. In some cases the car wouldn't run because the valve was jammed in the open position, a few times the airbox (see picture #100) had blown anyway, and one car had a really interesting problem. Poor top end performance was the complaint, which simply means the car did not accelerate well above 4,000 rpm. We were not aware that this car had been fitted with a pop off

Picture #100

valve, so we went through the normal sequence of events attempting to locate a problem. During this operation a strange whistle was heard from the airbox area when the car was revved quickly. We lifted off the air filter housing and filter insert and there it was, a pop off valve! Almost brand new and installed correctly, with a defective seal that allowed unmetered air to enter the engine during high rpm driving. This problem could easily have led to a burned piston, burned valves, or other problems, because the pop off valve, by design, has to be placed downstream from the fuel mixture unit, so the air leak was causing a very lean mixture in the engine. This, in turn, causes extremely high combustion chamber temperatures that the engine cannot cope with. With the improvements made to the airboxes by Porsche, there is absolutely no need for an add-on device such as this.

Picture #101

Reproduction wheels come in a wide variety of quality levels, and some aftermarket wheels, BBS products, for example, are outstanding, but some wheels are manufactured to look like the traditional five spoke factory alloy wheel. Unlike the factory wheel, these wheels are cast, not forged, which may give them an inherent weakness. We have seen two cases where control of a car was lost, on the street, and after sliding into a curb, the factory wheels would have bent, allowing the car to cross the curb and stop without serious damage. With the reproduction wheels, and the same scenario, the wheels broke (as in the example in picture #101), causing the car to dig in from sudden air loss, and actually flip the car over on its roof! When purchasing a car that has wheels fitted that appear to be factory alloys, always be sure to check the back side of the wheel for the eleven digit Porsche part number imprinted on the inside surface of one of the five spokes. If there are no numbers, you're looking at a cheap reproduction.

Rebuilt clutches are not a common item in the Porsche market, and are an item to definitely stay away from.

A host of short shift kits have appeared in the market place over the last few years. These kits were produced to satisfy those of us that always felt that the shift throw on 1973 and later 911s was too long. Be aware that the percentage figures for shifter movement claimed by some manufacturers are greatly exaggerated. Also, some just don't shift well because of manufacturer design. Like most other aftermarket items, the cost has to be kept way down or the item won't sell well, so one ends up with a product that's not quite right. Rest easy, now the shift throw can be shortened on all 1973 and later models, using factory parts. In 1985 the Carrera was fitted, as a standard item, with a shifter that reduced shift throw by 10% over all previous models. Porsche also introduced their short shift option kit, designated M241, about the same time, and is available from Porsche dealers under the factory part number 911 424 931 00. Both will retrofit, but the M241 has a stiffer motion, and shifting characteristics for both are terrific. One last note on shifters, be sure to contact a Porsche Club of America member and borrow their May, 1987 issue of Panorama, because this issue contains the most comprehensive article that's been written concerning short shift kits to date.

Finally, when dealing in the segment of the aftermarket that is intended to "improve" the Porsche automobile, restraint is necessary and homework is mandatory, because these pieces rarely ever work correctly, or have a long life expectancy.

Conclusion

Porsche 911 production, from 1964 through 1998, has certainly had its ups and downs. However, even the products of the worst 911 years, in mint condition, are still probably better all around cars than just about anything an equal number of dollars can buy brand new from a different marque.

The 911 seemed to hit bottom with the 1972 T and the 1975 S, while attaining near perfection with the 1967 S, 1970 and 1971 T and S, 1973 CIS fuel injected T, most 911 SC models and the 1988 and 1989 Carreras. The 993 model range, by all indications, will also earn its rightful place among the other top dogs of Porsche production history. The lows have all had a lot to do with meeting emissions standards, while the highs just seem to happen. In between the highs and lows are a myriad of models to choose from, with an astonishing number of options and standard equipment, depending on the year of the car.

The most important possession to take with you when you begin your hunt for a used 911 is patience. The second most important item is this manual. Don't forget it when your search for possibly the second or third most expensive thing you'll ever purchase begins. Good luck and many happy miles of motoring in your new-used Porsche 911!

Bibliography

(Author uncredited) Technical Specification Booklet, 1965 - 1968. Porsche AG, Stuttgart - Zuffenhausen, West Germany, 1976.

(Author uncredited) Technical Specification Booklet, 1969 - 1971. Porsche AG, Stuttgart - Zuffenhausen, West Germany, 1971.

(Author uncredited) Technical Specification Booklet, 1972 - 1973. Porsche AG, Stuttgart - Zuffenhausen, West Germany, 1973.

(Author uncredited) Technical Specification Booklet, 1974. Porsche AG, Stuttgart - Zuffenhausen, West Germany, 1974.

(Author uncredited) Technical Specification Booklet, 1975. Porsche AG, Stuttgart - Zuffenhausen, West Germany, 1977.

(Author uncredited) Technical Specification Booklet, 1976 - 1977. Porsche AG, Stuttgart - Zuffenhausen, West Germany, 1977.

(Author uncredited) Technical Specification Booklet, 1978 - 1981. Porsche AG, Stuttgart - Zuffenhausen, West Germany, 1981.

(Author uncredited) Technical Specification Booklet, 1982 - 1983. Porsche AG, Stuttgart - Zuffenhausen, West Germany, 1987.

(Author uncredited) Technical Specification Booklet, 1984 - 1987. Porsche AG, Stuttgart - Zuffenhausen, West Germany, 1986.

(Author uncredited) Technical Information, Carrera/Turbo, 1988. Porsche AG, Stuttgart - Zuffenhausen, West Germany, 1987.

(Author uncredited) Technical Information, Carrera/Turbo, 1989. Porsche AG, Stuttgart - Zuffenhausen, West Germany, 1988.

(Author uncredited) Technical Information, Carrera4, 1989. Porsche AG, Stuttgart - Zuffenhausen, West Germany, 1988.

Bruce Anderson. Porsche 911 Performance Handbook, Motorbooks International, Osceloa, WI., USA, 1987.

Bob Gagnon, Porsche Panorama, Porsche Club of America, Atlanta Georgia, USA May, 1988

Karl Ludvigsen, Porsche, Excellence Was Expected, Princeton Publishing, Inc., Princeton, NJ, 1977

(Author uncredited) Service Information Technik, 911 Turbo 3.6, 1993, Porsche AG, Stuttgart - Zuffenhausen, Germany, 1992.

(Author uncredited) Service Information Technik, 911/Turbo, 1997, Porsche AG, Stuttgart - Zuffenhausen, Germany, 1996.

Purchasing a second-hand Porsche 911 can be, and often is, a pleasant experience full of high expectations for the future. However, far too many times, this experience has ended with a shattered dream when the engine blows, or the rust in the chassis is found, or the heavy structural damage from the head-on collision is located. When this happens, a bitter taste can be left in one's mouth in regard to Porsches in general. This is the worst situation of all because I am convinced that the Porsche 911 really is the world's best car, and I am saddened deeply after talking to someone who has a genuine dislike for the marque because he unknowingly bought someone else's problems.This manual was written with the sincere hope that it will provide the reader with enough information to make an intelligent decision on whether to buy or not to buy. Sellers beware! The person you're trying to sell your "rust bucket" to just may have a copy of this book in his pocket.